IRREFUTABLE

EVIDENCE

Mathematical and Scientific Proof

The Bible is From God

DONNA CASTER

All quoted English scripture in the text of this book is from *The NIV StudyBible New International Version*, Zondervan Bible Publishers, 1985, unless otherwise noted.

7710-T Cherry Park Dr, Ste 224 Houston, TX 77095
(713) 766-4271

Cover design by Teresa Granberry, www.HarvestCreek.net

Printed in the United States of America

ISBN: 978-1-64830-325-8

Dear Venessa,

The Lord bless you and keep you;
the Lord make His face shine on you
and be gracious to you;
the Lord turn His face toward you
and give you peace.

— Numbers 6:24-26

Donna S. Caster
7/17/2021
DonnaCaster@me.com
DonnasBooks.com

What People are Saying about this Book

"For decades I have known and preached on the significance of numbers in the Bible. *Irrefutable Evidence* opens a whole new dimension of God's numerical design in the Scriptures. The numerical connection of the living and active Word of God to the DNA of all living things is incredible. Everyone who reads this book will probably say the same thing: 'Wow!'"

- Troy Brewer, Senior Pastor at Open Door Church in Burleson, Texas and author of over ten books including *Numbers that Preach* and *Redeeming Your Timeline*

"This amazing book offered to me a new realm of evidence that the Bible is divinely inspired. It presents the astonishing mathematical design behind the Scriptures—an intelligent design which cannot possibly be attributed to mere coincidence. Along with the evidence of countless fulfilled prophecies from Scripture as well as miraculous healings, any skeptic who seeks out the truth based on these facts will be convinced that the Bible is from the One True God."

- Pastors William & Lucille Lau, Founders of The Elijah Challenge and authors of *Dancing on the Edge of the Earth*

"If the Creator of the universe can create the heavens and the earth out of absolutely nothing, and speak it into existence, then it makes sense that He has the creative genius and power to orchestrate the original Hebrew and Greek scriptures into a creative, mystifying marvel of wonder. Donna Caster's *Irrefutable Evidence* provides a wonder of God's gifting in her volume providing one with a reason to believe. I encourage anyone to read this revelation who would question the Bible's accuracy, inspiration and reliability. Numbers keep us honest."

- Dr. Dennis Lindsay, President Christ for the Nations Institute and author of over 20 books including *Nature Speaks of Intelligent Design*

"*Irrefutable Evidence* will help anyone with misconceptions about the Bible to know that indeed it is from God. I believe that this book will help people of many different countries to look at the Bible in a different way. The fact that the Bible has mathematical design is of supreme importance for skeptics to understand the truth about our Creator. The evidence presented in this book proves the Bible is trustworthy as coming from the heart of God, not from the hearts of man. It is the written Word of God. I whole heartedly endorse this book and encourage people everywhere to examine the evidence."

- Katherine Hines, Hines Ugandan Ministries and author of *They Call Me Momma Katherine*

"*Irrefutable Evidence* is a stunning revelation of the intricate mathematical design of both the Old and New Testaments. People all over the world need to know the truth presented that the Bible is not only *about* God, but *from* God.

We read in the Bible that Wisemen from the east followed the star to come and worship Jesus, and Shepherds got the message of Jesus' birth through an angel and they went to see Jesus. This tells us that God loves both the intellectuals and the common men, and He communicates His love to everyone in a way that they can understand.

Irrefutable Evidence will convince many intellectuals and common people around the world that the Bible is not only about God, but from God Himself. I was blessed and challenged by the personal experiences and testimony of the Author in the last few chapters. I'm sure people from various nations, including India, will find this book very interesting and empowering. I appreciate Ms. Donna Caster for her hard work and deep research she has done in various fields to write this amazing book. I whole-heartedly endorse this book and encourage people everywhere to examine the evidence."

- Dr. Jebasingh Dhanaraj, India

"As a Muslim Background Believer, I recognize that many people around the world believe that the Bible has been corrupted. However, anyone who reads *Irrefutable Evidence* will be unable to deny the intentional mathematical design of both the Old and New Testaments. Along with other evidences presented of prophecy and miracles, one will be able to see that the Bible is a gift to us from our Creator God. If anyone reads *Irrefutable Evidence* with a pure heart, they will discover the Truth of the Word of God and the Hope of Eternal Life through Jesus Christ."

- Saleim Kahleh, SKMinistries.org

"Donna Caster lays out the case why the Bible is not just a book about God, but is divinely inspired by God and should be taken seriously. If you're a doubter, a skeptic, or already a believer who just wants the added assurance of how God did and still works things together according to His wisdom and purpose, read this book. Examine the facts, hear the witnesses, and be persuaded by *Irrefutable Evidence*."

- Justin Oneacre, Senior Pastor, Freedom House and author of *A Champion's Path*

"The numerical evidence, prophetic evidence, miraculous evidence and personal testimony in *Irrefutable Evidence* is overwhelmingly convincing that the Bible is indeed inspired by God. It is my prayer that this book will ignite a curiosity in all nations to discover the truth of the Bible."

- John Lewis, Founder of Ignite Ministries, www.igniteministry.org

CONTENTS

This verse continues to show the mathematical signs God has hidden in His Word with undeniable links to Genesis 1:1 and the DNA in all living things.

The creation of mankind in the image of God stated in Genesis 1:27 and Genesis 2:23 has incredible connection to our DNA and the number of chromosomes in human beings. Undeniable evidence of intelligent design in these scriptures.

Key New Testament verses that claim "in Him all things hold together", "sustaining all things by His powerful Word", "not the smallest letter of the Word will disappear until everything is accomplished" and others are shown to have direct correlation with our DNA.

This chapter is devoted to John 3:16 and the amazing mathematical connection to Genesis 1:1 and our DNA.

The mathematical phenomena of the I AM statements in the Old Testament and the New Testament give surprising evidence that the entire Bible is inspired by God.

Section 2 - The Evidence of Prophecy

Astounding detailed prophecies about coming kingdoms, political alliances and marriages from the time of the Babylonian Captivity until nearly the time of Christ, a period of about 600 years, all prophesied in Scripture and reviewable from Historical Record outside the Bible.

The major prophecies of Messiah as the Suffering Servant and Savior of our Sins is revealed in comparison with Old Testament Prophecies and New Testament fulfillment.

The amazing prophecies scattered throughout the Old Testament that the Jewish people would be restored to their Promised Land in Israel after being scattered to nations all over the earth. These prophecies from over 2400 years ago are being fulfilled right now in our life time!

Section 3 - The Evidence of Miracles and Personal Testimony

A look at several modern-day documented miracles that indicate the miraculous, supernatural events recorded in the Bible are not fiction, but actual miracles.

Personal Testimony of miraculous workings of God in my life through divine intervention, personal Word from God through the Bible, angelic help, supernatural miracles, overcoming demonic attack and peace in difficult trials.

Putting it all together, this book demonstrates irrefutable evidence that the Bible is not only a book about God, but from God.

INTRODUCTION

A couple of years ago I happened to see an article on the Internet that Genesis 1:1 has a mathematical pattern of sevens discovered by a man name Ivan Panin.[1] Ivan immigrated to the United States from Russia in 1877 when he was 22, and earned a Master's Degree from Harvard University in Literary Criticism. He was a firm agnostic, but after discovering some numerical patterns in the Hebrew scriptures of the Old Testament and the Greek language of the New Testament, he became a believer in God. He realized that the numerical patterns were designed and hidden into the scripture, not circumstantially random. His conversion to Christianity at the age of 35 made newspaper headlines. He shared his findings and conversion to Christianity in his book, *The Structure of the Bible: A Proof of the Verbal Inspiration of Scripture*, published in 1891.[2]

The article I stumbled on shows that Genesis 1:1 in the original Hebrew has a designed structure of "sevens". There are seven Hebrew words in this verse, 49 letters and 30 different combinations of "sevens" that Ivan discovered in the one verse. He presented his findings to the Mathematics Department at Harvard and challenged the professors to creatively design a sentence in the English language on any subject that would have similar patterns of sevens. They could not do it. This discovery of numerical design in Genesis 1:1 led Ivan to spend the next 50 years of his life researching the mathematical patterns imbedded in the Scripture which reveal intelligent design of the Bible.

The mathematical and numerical design in the Bible is intriguing due to factual numbers that correspond to the text as I will show, step by step. The mathematical phenomena are not something that could have been designed by the human writers of the Bible, as you will see. Since Hebrew and Greek letters correspond to numbers, it is possible to see numerical design and mathematical formulas that link verses from the Old Testament (Tanakh) and the New Testament with undeniable precision and intentional, intelligent design.

Additionally, by breaking down the DNA molecules of all living things into the number of protons and neutrons in each molecule, there is astounding correlation between the numbers associated with DNA and numbers associated with numerous verses throughout the Bible. The correlation is so solid and clear, it is undoubtedly the result of intelligent, intentional design. The mathematical and numerical patterns and data I will show you are irrefutable evidence the Bible is divinely inspired. It is not only a book about God, but a book from the Eternal God.

Although the numerical evidence is the heart of this book, I will also highlight three groupings of prophecies in the Old Testament (Tanakh) that have already been fulfilled:

1) Prophecies in Daniel concerning world history from the time of the Babylonian Empire to the time of Jesus Christ,

2) Prophecies throughout the Old Testament concerning the coming of Jesus Christ, the Messiah, in his role as Savior of mankind from sin, and

3) Prophecies throughout the Old Testament concerning the restoration of Israel as a nation.

Prophecy is supernatural and is another evidence the Bible is divinely inspired. The detail and clarity of fulfilled prophetic words written hundreds and thousands of years beforehand in the Bible is amazing.

Some people discredit the Bible as fiction because of the miracles recorded in it. I also have devoted a section to modern-day, documented, undeniable miracles that can be examined. I have selected miracles with detailed, documented data that can be investigated: miraculous instantaneous healings, incredible stories of survival, and other examples of Biblical-type miracles happening today. Since miracles still happen today, they certainly happened, as recorded thousands of years ago in the Bible.

Finally, I will share my own personal testimony how I have experienced the Bible as a supernatural book, experienced miracles in my own life, and have connected with our Creator in so many wonderful ways.

For those interested in a few basic facts about the Bible:

- The Bible consists of 66 books written by 40 persons (30 in the Old Testament and 10 in the New Testament) over 1500 years, from mid-14th century BC to first century AD.
- The thread of the Bible is consistent even though written by 40 different people over 1500 years.
- The 66 books of the Bible are referred to as the "Canon", the books regarded as inspired by God. (See biblica.com FAQ #7 for more information on how the Canon was chosen.)
- Jesus referred to the Old Testament books as "scripture", which means "inspired". He quoted verses of scripture from 24 books of the Old Testament.
- 99.6% of the New Testament has been corroborated by other historical documents.[3]
- The Bible has been translated into more languages than any other book. According to Wycliffe Global Alliance, as of October 2020 the complete Bible has been translated into 704 languages, the New Testament into 1551 languages and at least some Scripture has been translated for 3415 languages.[4]

Getting to know the heart of God through the reading of His Word has been the highest blessing of my life. It is my earnest desire to help others recognize truth, the Bible is God's love letter to humanity. For some people, understanding God did give us a hidden mathematical code in the Scripture, is just what they may need to believe the Bible is from the Creator-God, not human origin.

SECTION 1

MATHEMATICAL DESIGN
IN THE SCRIPTURES

CHAPTER 1

Original Languages of the Bible

In order to look at the mathematical evidence of intelligent design of the Bible, you have to look at the original language. The Bible is made up of two main sections: the Old Testament (Tanakh) and the New Testament. The Old Testament was written predominantly in Hebrew, and the New Testament was written in Greek. Please see more detailed information about the original languages of scripture in Appendix 1.

Hebrew and Greek Letter and Number Equivalents

The Hebrew alphabet has 22 letters of consonant sounds. Five of the letters have a modified form when the letter ends a word. There is not an upper-case and lower-case form of the letters. Hebrew is different from English since it is written from right to left.

The Greek alphabet has more similarity to English in that it has 24 letters, (26 characters in the English alphabet), with upper and lower case letters, and is written from left to right. The earliest Greek manuscripts of the New Testament were written with all upper-case letters.

Both Hebrew and Greek alphabets represent numbers and letters. Prior to the usage of the numerical digits—1, 2, 3, 4, 5, 6, 7, 8, 9, 0—numbers were assigned to the specific letters of the alphabet. Numbers as we use them today originated in India about the 6th century and were introduced to Europe through the writings of Middle Eastern mathematicians about the 12th century.[1] But before that, letters of the alphabet were used for both letters and numbers.

So, for example, the first letter of the Hebrew alphabet, Aleph = 1 and the first letter of the Greek alphabet, Alpha = 1. The second letter equals 2, the tenth letter equals 10. Then the 11th letter equals 20, rather than 11 because 11 can be expressed by 10 + 1. The 12th letter equals 30, etc. Larger numbers are expressed by a combination of letters. Table 1 shows the Hebrew letter and number equivalents and Table 2 shows the Greek letter and number equivalents.

Table 1. Hebrew Letter and Number Equivalents

Hebrew	Letter	Number	Hebrew	Letter	Number	Hebrew	Letter	Number
Aleph	א	1	Yud	י	10	Qof	ק	100
Bet/Vet	ב	2	Kaf	כ	20	Resh	ר	200
Gimmel	ג	3	Lamed	ל	30	Shin/Sin	ש	300
Dalet	ד	4	Mem	מ	40	Tav	ת	400
Hey	ה	5	Nun	נ	50	Kaf (final)	ך	20 or 500
Vav	ו	6	Samech	ס	60	Mem (final)	ם	40 or 600
Zayin	ז	7	Ayin	ע	70	Nun (final)	ן	50 or 700
Chet	ח	8	Pey/Fey	פ	80	Pey (final)	ף	80 or 800
Tet	ט	9	Tzadi	צ	90	Tzadi (final)	ץ	90 or 900

If you notice the final form of the last five letters in Table 1 have two different numbers that they can represent. For the purposes of the mathematical intelligent design I will show of the scriptures in this book, I use the same number equivalent for the letter whether it is used at the beginning or within a word, or as a final form. For example, the letter Kaf is equivalent to 20 whether it is used at the beginning, middle or end of a word.

Table 2. Greek Letter and Number Equivalents

Greek	Letter	Number	Greek	Letter	Number	Greek	Letter	Number
Alpha	A	1	Iota	I	10	Rho	P	100
Beta	B	2	Kappa	K	20	Sigma	Σ	200
Gamma	Γ	3	Lamda	Λ	30	Tau	T	300
Delta	Δ	4	Mu	M	40	Upsilon	Y	400
Epsilon	E	5	Nu	N	50	Phi	Φ	500
Zeta	Z	7	Xi	Ξ	60	Chi	X	600
Eta	H	8	Omicron	O	70	Psi	Ψ	700
Theta	Θ	9	Pi	Π	80	Omega	Ω	800

In Table 2, you may notice there is no letter equivalent for the number 6 or the number 90. In ancient Greek, there used to be a letter in the Greek alphabet called wau or digamma which represented the number 6, but it was later dropped from the alphabet in the Byzantine era.[2] Likewise, the Greek letter Qoppa (upper case Q) is also an obsolete letter of the Greek alphabet which became extinct by pre-Classical times (800-500 BC).[3]

Since the letters also represent numbers, it is possible to assign each word an equivalent number by adding up all the individual letters of the word. This practice is called *gematria*. The gematria of each word or phrase can be significant, as well as the gematria of an entire verse. With this foundation let's get started to understand the mathematical evidence of divine inspiration of the scriptures. And the best place to start is, "in the beginning."

CHAPTER 2

Genesis 1:1

With the background of the previous chapter, we are now ready to begin our journey of discovery. Beware, be prepared to be blown away! The Bible is organized by books, chapters and verses. The very first book of the Old Testament is Genesis. Genesis has 50 "chapters," and each of these chapters is made up of verses. So, whenever anyone refers to a particular verse of the Bible, it is the *Book, ChapterNumber: VerseNumber*. So, the first verse of the Bible is

"In the beginning God created the heavens and the earth."[1]

— Genesis 1:1

This verse tells us that we have a creator, God. The heavens, the earth, all of the elements that make up the earth, our atmosphere, and every living thing on the earth was intricately created by God. What I'm going to show you is the verse itself, in Hebrew, has definitive, intelligent, mathematical design that could not just be coincidental or even orchestrated by the human being, Moses, who wrote the words.

First, let's look at the structural phenomena of "sevens" in the verse. Figure 1 shows the Hebrew letters and words of this verse. Remember that Hebrew reads right to left.

7 6 5 4 3 2 1

28 27 26 25 24 23 22 21 20 19 18 17 16 15 14 13 12 11 10 9 8 7 6 5 4 3 2 1

בְּרֵאשִׁית בָּרָא אֱלֹהִים אֵת הַשָּׁמַיִם וְאֵת הָאָרֶץ׃

B'resheet bara Elohim et ha-shem-ayim ve'et ha-aretz

In the beginning God created the heavens and the earth.

Figure 1. Genesis 1:1 in Hebrew and English with letter and word count.[2]

There are seven key structural elements of the verse that reveal a pattern of sevens through the word and letter combinations:

1. There are seven Hebrew words that make up the verse.
2. There are 28 Hebrew letters that make up the verse, a multiple of seven (7x4).
3. The third and fourth words combined have seven letters.
4. The fourth and fifth words combined have seven letters.
5. The sixth and seventh words combined have seven letters.
6. The first three words have 14 letters, which is a multiple of seven (7x2).
7. The remaining four words have 14 letters.

Figure 2 shows the numerical equivalents of each letter and the associated gematria of each word, by adding up all the letters of each word. The top number is the gematria of the word, and the numbers immediately above the letters are the numbers associated with each letter. Remembering that Hebrew is written from right to left, the first word is on the far right and the seventh word of this verse is on the far left.

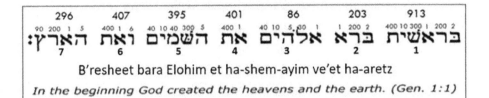

296	407	395	401	86	203	913

Figure 2. Genesis 1:1 in Hebrew and English showing the numerical
equivalents of each letter and word.

By assigning the numerical equivalent to each letter and determining
the gematria of each word, there are some additional structural elements of
sevens:

- The numeric value of the second word is 203, which is a multiple of
  seven (29 x 7).

- The sum of the first and last letters of all seven words is 1393, which
  equals 199 x 7 (2+400 + 2+1 + 1+40 + 1+400 + 5+40 + 6+400 +
  5+90).

- The sum of the first and last letters of the first and last words is 497,
  which equals 71 x 7 (2+400 + 5+90).

Before moving on, I'd like to share a little bit about the number seven and
how it is significant in the Bible. The number "7" is significant because it
represents spiritual perfection and completeness. There are seven days in a
week. As recorded in Genesis 2, God created the world in six days, rested on
the seventh, and blessed the seventh day and made it holy.

*By the seventh day God had finished the work He had been
doing; so on the seventh day He rested from all His work. And
God blessed the seventh day and made it holy, because on it he
rested from all the work of creating that he had done.*

— Genesis 2:2-3

To debate whether these days are literal 24-hour days or seven periods of time is not the purpose of this book. However, it is a stumbling block to some and the Bible is immediately discredited as fiction since it is believed in the scientific community that the earth is 4.5 billion years old. It is important to get over this stumbling block because the important truth is that God created us, the heavens and the earth. The literal amount of time it took is not relevant. I believe that time in eternity is completely different than time on earth. Also, keep in mind that there are an infinite number of numbers between 0 and 1. There is 1/0.9999999999 and on to infinity, as well as ½, ¼, 1/8, 1/16, and on to infinity. Time, as we know it on earth is most likely not the same as time when God created the heavens and the earth. The intricate details of how God created the world is not disclosed in the Bible. What is hidden in the first verse of the Bible is that the sentence has a structural component of sevens, purposefully designed into the verse.

There is *much* more mathematical phenomena hidden in Genesis 1:1. Moving on, if you add all the words together, you get the gematria of the entire verse which is 2701.

$$913 + 203 + 86 + 401 + 395 + 407 + 296 = 2701$$

Here is where things start getting interesting. At first glance, there is nothing seemingly special about the number 2701. However, let's dissect this number. The factors of 2701 are 1, 37, 73, 2701. Some interesting phenomena of the number 2701 are listed below:[3]

- $37 \times 73 = 2701$. Interestingly 37 and 73 are reflective.

- 37 is the 12th prime number and 73 is the 21st prime number. 12 and 21 are also reflective.

- Placing 37 and 73 together as the number 3773 = 7 x 7 x 77.

- Placing 12 and 21 together as the number 1221 = 37 x 3.

There are also some geometrical phenomena with the numbers 2701,

37 and 73. Remember 2701 = 37 x 73. Triangles, hexagons and stars make up shapes utilizing these three numbers. Let me explain first by looking at triangular numbers. Figure 3 shows the first four triangular numbers.

O O O O	1st Triangular number = 1
OO OO OO	2nd Triangular number = 3
OOO OOO	3rd Triangular number = 6
OOOO	4th Triangular number = 10

Figure 3. The first four triangular numbers.

The first triangular number is one. The second triangular number is three because it has a base of two plus one circle (in the example above) to make a total of three circles in the shape of a triangle. The third triangular number is six because it has a base of three circles, then above that two circles, then above that one circle to make the triangle. Counting all the circles, gives six. The fourth triangular number has a base of 4, then 3, then 2, then 1, forming a triangle. The fourth triangular number is 10 because 4 + 3 + 2 + 1 = 10. The formula for triangular numbers is $n(n+1)/2$. Plugging in **73** for n gives **2701**. That means a triangle with a base of 73 circles/dots, then the next line up contains 72 circles/dots, then 71, all the way up to one, add up all the circles/dots and you get 2701. Simply speaking,

- The 73rd triangular number is 2701.

Genesis 1:1 also has a triangular symmetry with the 37th triangular number.

- The 37th triangular number is 703, which is what the 6th and 7th words sum to, 407 + 296 = 703.

The remaining words of Genesis 1:1, words 1 – 5, add up to 1998 (913 + 203 + 86 + 401 + 395). 1998 = 666 x 3 and 666 is the 36th triangular number. In visual form, you can take the three triangles of base 36, the 36th triangular number which equals 666, and the triangle that makes up the

37th triangular number and make one large triangle that is equivalent to a base of 73, the 73rd triangular number, which equals 2701.[4] It's confusing to describe in words, but picture it below in Figure 4.

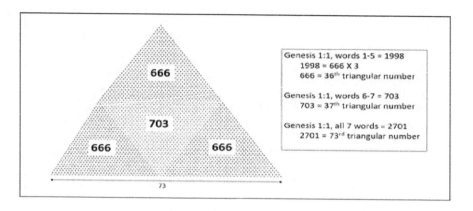

Figure 4. Triangular structural unity in Genesis 1:1.

There is mathematical structural unity to Genesis 1:1 with these triangular numbers that come from the gematria of the verse.

I recognize "666" is the number of the AntiChrist (Revelation 13:18). May this book help people discover the truth of the Lord Jesus Christ and have nothing to do with the AntiChrist. I include the geometric structure of Genesis 1:1 with three triangles of "666" simply as a geometrical phenomenon of the verse.

Another interesting triangular number that is in Genesis 1:1 is the 7th triangular number. The 7th triangular number is 28. Genesis 1:1 has 7 words and 28 letters.

There is additional geometrical structural unity in this verse as well with hexagonal numbers. Figure 5 shows the first four hexagonal numbers.

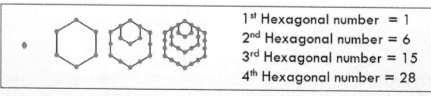

Figure 5. The first four hexagonal numbers.

The first hexagonal number is one. The second hexagonal number is six because there are six points in a hexagon. The third hexagonal number consists of two hexagons sharing one point with additional points midway between the first hexagon. Adding up all the points comes to 15. The formula for hexagonal numbers is n(2n-1). Plugging in **37** for n gives **2701**.

- The 37th hexagonal number is 2701.

There is also structural unity with the numbers 37, 73 and 2701, the gematria of Genesis 1:1, with star numbers. Figure 6 shows the first four star numbers.

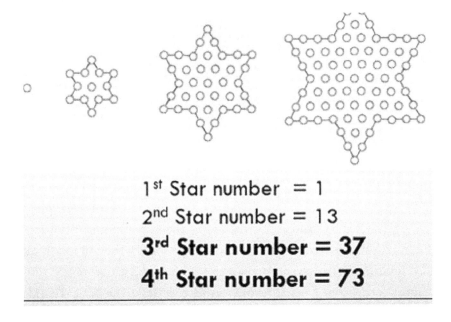

1st Star number = 1
2nd Star number = 13
3rd **Star number = 37**
4th **Star number = 73**

Figure 6. The first four star numbers.

The first star number is one. The second star number is thirteen because there are thirteen dots that make up the star with one dot in the middle. The third star number is equal to 37 and the fourth star number is equal to 73.

Lastly, 37 and 73 is a hexagon/star pair. In Figure 7 below there are 37 circles that make up the hexagon and 73 circles that make up the star.

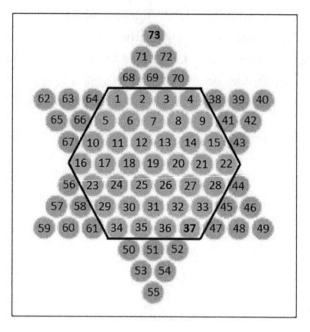

Figure 7. Hexagon and star showing 37 / 73 pair.

Thus, you can see that geometrically the number 2701, which equals 37 x 73 has geometrical unity in triangular numbers, hexagonal numbers and star numbers.

If we go back to the overall structure of the verse in terms of letters and words, we can see 3 7 and 7 3 (37 x 73) in the letter count of the second through sixth words. The second word has three letters, the third and fourth words combined have seven letters, the fourth and fifth words combined have seven letters and the sixth word has three letters. The 3 7 (37) and 7 3 (73) structure is shown in Figure 8 below.

Figure 8. Three – Seven, Seven – Three (37 x 73) pattern in the 2nd through 6th words of Genesis 1:1.

So, 37 and 73 are significant numbers in Genesis 1:1 since the gematria of Genesis 1:1 is 2701 and 2701 = 37 x 73. Does the Bible reveal any other significance to the numbers 37 and 73? First let's examine the number 37. There are 49 (7 x 7) words in the Bible that have a gematria of 37.[5] Appendix 2 shows these 49 words. There are nine words in Genesis with a gematria of 37, two words in Exodus, two words in Numbers, two words in Judges, two words in 1 Samuel, three words in 1&2 Kings, one word in 2 Chronicles, three words in Ezra, one word in Esther, two words in Job, six words in Psalms, one word in Isaiah, five words in Jeremiah, two words in Lamentations, two words in Daniel, one word in Jonah, one word in Habakkuk, and one word in Zechariah. In all, 46 words in the Old Testament with a gematria of 37. Then there are three words in the New Testament with a gematria of 37, one in Matthew, Mark and Hebrews, for a total of 49 words in the Bible with a gematria of 37.

Previously I shared the significance of the number seven to be spiritual perfection and completeness. The number 37, which is an integral part of Genesis 1:1 is located throughout the Bible in 49 (7 x 7) different places and 21 (3 x 7) different books. (Note: the Jewish Tanakh, equivalent to the Christian Old Testament, considers 1&2 Kings as one book.) These 49 words in 21 different books that have a gematria of 37 indicate that the entire Bible is from God, designed intentionally with spiritual perfection and completeness.

What about the number 73? Is there any special significance in the scripture to this number? In Hebrew, the word, chokmah, means wisdom and has a gematria of 73.

5+40+20+8=73

חכמה

5 40 20 8

One key scripture with this word, wisdom, that connects the creation to the wisdom of the Lord is in Proverbs.

*By **wisdom** the LORD laid the earth's foundations, by understanding He set the heavens in place.*

— Proverbs 3:19

An interesting point about the gematria of the Hebrew word for wisdom is that if you take the ordinal value of the word, the gematria is 37. Table 1 shows the standard numerical equivalents of the Hebrew letters along with the ordinal numerical equivalents of the Hebrew letters.

Table 1. Standard and Ordinal Numeric Values of Hebrew Letters

Hebrew	Letter	Standard	Ordinal	Hebrew	Letter	Standard	Ordinal	Hebrew	Letter	Standard	Ordinal
Aleph	א	1	1	Yud	י	10	10	Qof	ק	100	19
Bet/Vet	ב	2	2	Kaf	כ	20	11	Resh	ר	200	20
Gimmel	ג	3	3	Lamed	ל	30	12	Shin/Sin	שׁ	300	21
Dalet	ד	4	4	Mem	מ	40	13	Tav	ת	400	22
Hey	ה	5	5	Nun	נ	50	14	Kaf (final)	ך	20	11
Vav	ו	6	6	Samech	ס	60	15	Mem (final)	ם	40	13
Zayin	ז	7	7	Ayin	ע	70	16	Nun (final)	ן	50	14
Chet	ח	8	8	Pey/Fey	פ	80	17	Pey (final)	ף	80	17
Tet	ט	9	9	Tzadi	צ	90	18	Tzadi (final)	ץ	90	18

The standard numerical value for the Hebrew word, chokmah is 73, but the ordinal value is 37.

$$5+13+11+8=37$$

חכמה

5   13   11   8

So far I have shown multiple patterns of "sevens" in the first verse of the Bible, and special phenomenon with the gematria of Genesis 1:1, 2701 = 37 x 73. Still, we have only just barely begun with mathematical phenomena in this first verse of the Bible. There are other interesting phenomena when you add the gematria of certain words together:[6]

- The sum of the 3rd + 5th + 7th words = 86 + 395 + 296 = **777** = **37 x 7 x 3**

- The sum of the 3rd + 5th + 6th words = 86 + 395 + 407 =**888** = **37 x 8 x 3**

- The sum of the 1st + 3rd words = 913 + 86 = **999** = **37 x 9 x 3**

- The sum of the 2nd + 4th + 5th words = 203 + 401 + 395 = **999** = **37 x 9 x 3**

Additionally, to a pattern of "sevens" in Genesis 1:1, there are patterns of 777, 888 and 999 in this verse as various words are added together. Each of these triplet digit numbers is a multiple of 37.

All of these geometrical, structural and numerical patterns in this first verse of the Bible is designed by the author of the verse. It could be random, perhaps, but not likely. However, as we investigate more mathematical phenomena of this verse, you will see it becomes increasingly less likely to be random, but most likely to be designed.

Next, I will reveal how applying a mathematical formula to Genesis 1:1 yields the mathematical constant π, pronounced "pi".[7] As shown in Figure 9, if you take the number of letters in Genesis 1:1 (28) and multiply 28 by the product of all the letters (2 x 200 x 300 x 10 x 400 x 2 x 200 x 30 x 5 x 10 x 40 x 400 x 5 x 300 x 40 x 10 x 40 x 6 x 400 x 5 x 200 x 90), then divide that number by the number of words of Genesis 1:1 (7) multiplied by the product of the words (913 x 203 x 86 x 401 x 395 x 407 x 296), you get 3.141×10^{17}. The number 3.141 is pi to the 3rd decimal place.

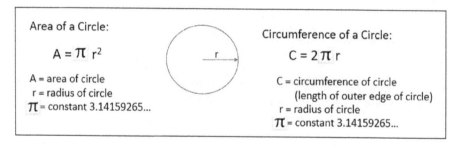

Figure 9. Mathematical Formula applied to Genesis 1:1 that gives the solution of pi.

For those who may not know the significance of π, it is the mathematical constant used to determine the area and circumference of a circle as shown in Figure 10.

Area of a Circle:

$$A = \pi \, r^2$$

A = area of circle
r = radius of circle
π = constant 3.14159265...

Circumference of a Circle:

$$C = 2 \pi \, r$$

C = circumference of circle
    (length of outer edge of circle)
r = radius of circle
π = constant 3.14159265...

Figure 10. Geometry of a circle using "pi" to determine the area and circumference of the circle.

The ancient Babylonians calculated the area of a circle by taking 3 times the square of its radius, which gave pi the value of three.

One Babylonian tablet (dated between 1900 – 1680 BC) indicates a value of 3.125 for Pi. Archimedes of Syracuse (287-212 BC) determined the approximate value of pi to be 3.1605.[8] Today we know that pi goes on for infinity. There is no EXACT number for pi. However, it is certain that Moses, the human author of Genesis, was not aware of the constant pi and did not design this mathematical phenomenon into this verse.

It is interesting to look at the numbers of pi beyond the decimal point in the Pi Tracker at www.angio.net/pi/piquery. This Pi Tracker has millions of digits of pi to the right of the decimal point so you can look for number sequences in pi. If you look for the string "999", it occurs for the first time at position 762 after the decimal (Figure 11). This first occurrence of "999" is followed by another "999". Just like you can find "999" twice in Genesis 1:1.

The string **999** occurs at position 762.
counting from the first digit after the decimal point. The 3. is not counted.

Find Next

The string and surrounding digits:

77130996051870721134   999   99983729780499510597

Figure 11. Pi Tracker showing the first occurrence of 999 after decimal point

The string "888" occurs in the Pi Tracker at position 4751 after the decimal point. It is followed by the numbers "800" (Figure 12).

The string **888** occurs at position 4751.
counting from the first digit after the decimal point. The 3. is not counted.

Find Next

The string and surrounding digits:

91807638327166416274   888   80078692560290228472

Figure 12. Pi Tracker showing the first occurrence of 888.

This is significant because the gematria for **Jesus** in Greek is 888 and the gematria for **Lord** in Greek is 800. And just for some additional information, the gematria for **Jesus Christ** in Greek is 888 + 1480 = 2368 = 37 x 8 x 8.

The Greek words for Lord Jesus Christ and associated gematria are listed below:

Lord	ΚΥΡΙΟΣ	800
Jesus	ΙΗΣΟΥΣ	888
Christ	ΧΡΙΣΤΟΣ	1480

The mathematical genius within Genesis 1:1 is irrefutable and undeniable. It is most assuredly a product of intentional design rather than coincidental chance. To summarize what has been covered so far in Genesis 1:1:

- Numerous patterns of sevens can be found in the verse.

- The gematria of the verse (the numeric equivalent of each letter added together for the entire verse) adds to 2701, which is a significant number for many reasons:

  o 2701 = 37 x 73
    * 37 and 73 are reflective
    * 37 is the 12th prime number and 73 is the 21st prime number
    * 12 and 21 are reflective
    * Placing 37 and 73 together to form the number 3773 = 7 x 7 x 77
    * Placing 12 and 21 together to form the number 1221 = 37 x 3
    * The 7th triangular number is 28 (Gen 1:1 has 7 words, 28 letters)
    * The 73rd triangular number is 2701

    * The 37th hexagonal number is 2701

    • The 3rd star number is 37 and the 4th star number is 73

    * The middle words of the verse, the 2nd, 3rd, 4th, 5th and

6th words give a pattern of 3 letters, 7 letters, 7 letters, 3 letters, again 3 7 and 7 3

- Triangular structural unit of the verse by taking

  o The gematria of the first 5 words is 1998, which his 666 x 3, where 666 is the 36th triangular number

  o The gematria of the 6th and 7th words is 703, which is the 37th triangular number

  o Placing the three triangles with base of 36 and the triangle with base of 37 together, forms one bigger triangle of base 73, the 73rd triangular number.

- There are 49 (7 x 7) words in the Bible in 21 (7 x 3) Books of the Bible that have a gematria of 37.

- The ordinal value of the Hebrew word for "wisdom" is 37 and the normal gematria for "wisdom" is 73.

- The sum of the 3rd + 5th + 7th words = 777 = 37 x 7 x 3, notice the 37 popping up again.

- The sum of the 3rd + 5th + 6th words = 888 = 37 x 8 x 3

- The sum of the 1st + 3rd words = 999 = 37 x 9 x 3

- The sum of the 2nd + 4th + 5th words = 999 = 37 x 9 x 3

- Applying a mathematical formula to Genesis 1:1 yields the constant pi.

- Using the pi tracker, the first occurrence of 999 occurs with a second 999 following.

- Using the pi tracker, the first occurrence of 888 occurs with 800 following. This is significant since 888 is the gematria for Jesus and 800 is the gematria for Lord.

Another amazing fact about Genesis 1:1, missed in the English translation, is the significance of the middle word. The middle word in Genesis 1:1 is a two-letter word that does not have a direct translation into English.

בראשית ברא אלהים את השמים ואת הארץ:

This word is made up of the Aleph, the first letter of the Hebrew alphabet, and the Tav, the last letter of the Hebrew alphabet. It is pronounced "et". In word for word translations from Hebrew to English, there is no equivalent English word; it is left untranslated in Genesis 1:1. The Interlinear Bible has the Hebrew words with the Strong's Concordance numbers that correlate to the English translation. There is no Strong's Concordance number for the word:

את

What is very interesting is, Jesus describes Himself as "*the Alpha and the Omega*", the first and last letters of the Greek alphabet, in Revelation 1:8, Revelation 21:6 and Revelation 22:13. I'd like to suggest, Jesus was actually quoting from Genesis 1:1 when he stated, "*I am the Alpha and the Omega*", which in Hebrew would have been the Aleph and the Tav, two letter middle word of Genesis 1:1. This word, Aleph-Tav symbolizes Jesus, who we will see in the next chapter is also referred to as the Word.

There are certainly many other evidences besides the mathematical phenomena found in Genesis 1:1 that we have a creator, and that the world we live in came into existence by intelligent design, not circumstantial chance. However, the mathematical discoveries in Genesis 1:1 gives factual evidence that this scripture was written with mathematical intelligent design beyond that of the human author. And since the verse speaks of creation, it is most logical that the imbedded mathematical patterns were incorporated in the written words from the Creator. Thus, this verse is inspired by God. It is not only *about* God, but *from* God.

CHAPTER 3

John 1:1

The New Testament verse like Genesis 1:1 is John 1:1, which states "*In the beginning was the Word and the Word was with God and the Word was God.*" The Greek rendition of John 1:1 is shown in Figure 1:

In the beginning was the Word	ΕΝ ΑΡΧΗΙ ΗΝ Ο ΛΟΓΟΣ
and the Word was with God	ΚΑΙ Ο ΛΟΓΟΣ ΗΝ ΠΡΟΣ ΤΟΝ ΘΕΟΝ
and God was the Word.	ΚΑΙ ΘΕΟΣ ΗΝ Ο ΛΟΓΟΣ

Figure 1. John 1:1 in Greek.

The first thing to note is the structure of this verse. Each phrase has a middle word of two letters, outlined in the boxes in Figure 2. The first and third lines have two words on either side of the middle word, and the 2nd line has three words on either side of the middle word. If you count the words and letters in each phrase of the verse, you can see a pattern of 5 - 7 - 5 words and 15 – 22 – 15 letters.

# Words	# Letters	
5	15	ΕΝ ΑΡΧΗΙ ‖ΗΝ‖ Ο ΛΟΓΟΣ
7	22	ΚΑΙ Ο ΛΟΓΟΣ ‖ΗΝ‖ ΠΡΟΣ ΤΟΝ ΘΕΟΝ
5	15	ΚΑΙ ΘΕΟΣ ‖ΗΝ‖ Ο ΛΟΓΟΣ

Figure 2. Structural pattern of John 1:1 with 2-letter middle word in each phrase

Genesis 1:1 also has a 2-letter middle word, with three words on either side (Figure 3):

Figure 3. Genesis 1:1 in Hebrew showing middle word with two letters.

It is noteworthy that scriptures with structural symmetry of letters and words are more likely to find a mathematical design within the scripture or phrase. For John 1:1, the gematria (numerical equivalent) of each word is shown in Figure 4 below[1]:

Interlinear English	Greek	Numeric value
in	EN	55
[the] beginning	APXHI	719
was	HN	58
the	O	70
Word	ΛΟΓΟΣ	373
and	KAI	31
the	O	70
Word	ΛΟΓΟΣ	373
was	HN	58
with	ΠΡΟΣ	450
	TON	420
God	ΘΕΟΝ	134
and	KAI	31
God	ΘΕΟΣ	284
was	HN	58
the	O	70
Word	ΛΟΓΟΣ	373

Figure 4. Gematria of John 1:1

Copies of New Testament Greek manuscripts do not all have the exact number of letters and words in some scriptures and it is much more difficult to get to the original Greek manuscripts than it is to get to the original Hebrew. The Jewish scribes meticulously kept the scriptures copied from generation to generation, word by word and letter by letter. However, there are numerous renditions of the Greek New Testament passages. There is an organization called Center for New Testament Restoration (CNTR), led by Dr. Alan Bunning, which works to identify the original Greek manuscripts.

I use the work of John Nuyten and his website https://livinggreeknt.org, along with CNTR for the Greek passages in this book. For example, the second word in John 1:1 is sometimes written as "APXH" instead of "APXHI" in some Greek manuscripts. However, the earliest Greek manuscript shows that this word contained the iota subscript as the last letter. In some later Greek manuscript copies the iota subscript was dropped. The original Greek, to the best of CNTR research is what I am using.

Back to John 1:1 and the gematria of each word as shown in Figure 4. If you add all words together the gematria of the entire verse is 3627. This is significant because 3627 = 39 x 93, another reflective pair similar to the 37 x 73, the gematria of Genesis 1:1. But there is much more connection of John 1:1 and Genesis 1:1.

As in Genesis 1:1, there are words that add up to 777, 888 and 999 in John 1:1. As shown in Figure 5 below, the second and third word, underlined with a solid line, add up to 777.

- 719 + 58 = 777

- 777 = **37** x **7** x **3**

The words underlined with square dots add up to 888. From the first line: 55+58+70, 70+58 +134 on the second line and 31+284+58+70 on the third line all add up to 888.

- 55+58+70+70+58+134+31+284+58+70= 888

- 888 = **37** x **8** x **3**

The words underlined in dashes add up to 999. From the first line: 55+70+373 and 70+373+58 on the second line add up to 999.

- 55+70+373+70+373+58=999

- 999 = **37** x **9** x **3**

There are two different combinations of numbers that equal 999 in Genesis 1:1. Similarly, with John 1:1, you can get a second set of numbers that add up to 999 by using the 70, 373 from the third line instead of the first line.

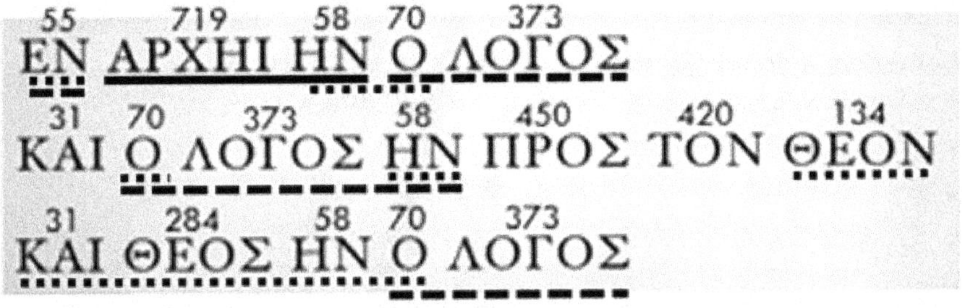

719+58 = 777

55+58+70+70+58+134+31+284+58+70 = 888

55+70+373+**70+373**+58 = 999 (from first phrase)

55+70+373+**70+373**+58 = 999 (from third phrase)

Figure 5. Words from John 1:1 that add to 777, 888 and 999.

It is also interesting to note that if you add the gematria of Genesis 1:1 and John 1:1, which is 2701 + 3627, you get 6328, which also happens to be a triangular number, the 112th triangular number.

But even more significantly, if you put the number of words and letters of John 1:1 into the same formula that showed that Genesis 1:1 gives the constant "pi", you get the constant "e" as shown below in Figure 6.[2]

$$\overset{55}{\text{EN}} \overset{719}{\text{APXHI}} \overset{58}{\text{HN}} \overset{70}{\text{O}} \overset{373}{\text{ΛΟΓΟΣ}}$$

$$\overset{31}{\text{KAI}} \overset{70}{\text{O}} \overset{373}{\text{ΛΟΓΟΣ}} \overset{58}{\text{HN}} \overset{450}{\text{ΠΡΟΣ}} \overset{420}{\text{TON}} \overset{134}{\text{ΘΕΟΝ}}$$

$$\overset{31}{\text{KAI}} \overset{284}{\text{ΘΕΟΣ}} \overset{58}{\text{HN}} \overset{70}{\text{O}} \overset{373}{\text{ΛΟΓΟΣ}}$$

$$\frac{\text{\# of letters X Product of letters}}{\text{\# of words X Product of words}} = \frac{52 \times (8.436 \times 10^{75})}{17 \times (9.493 \times 10^{35})} = 2.718 \times 10^{40}$$

$$e = 2.718$$

Figure 6. Formula applied to John 1:1 that gives the constant "e".

There are 52 Greek letters in John 1:1 and 17 words in John 1:1. If you plug in the gematria for each letter and each word you get 52 times the product of all the letters: ($\underline{5x50}$ x $\underline{1x100x600x8x10}$ x $\underline{8x50}$ x $\underline{70}$ x $\underline{30x70x3x70x200}$ x $\underline{20x1x10}$ x $\underline{70}$ x $\underline{30x70x3x70x200}$ x $\underline{8x50}$ x $\underline{80x100x70x200}$ x $\underline{300x70x50}$ x $\underline{9x5x70x50}$ x $\underline{20x1x10}$ x $\underline{9x5x70x200}$ x $\underline{8x50}$ x $\underline{70}$ x $\underline{30x70x3x70x200}$). Then divide this number by 17 x the product of all the words: (55 x 719 x 58 x 70 x 373 x 31 x 70 x 373 x 58 x 450 x 420 x 134 x 31 x 284 x 58 x 70 x 373). The solution of this equation is 2.718 x 10^{40}. The value of the constant "e" to the third decimal place is 2.718.

Don't let the significance of this pass you by. The number of letters and number of words for the first verse of the Bible, in Hebrew, which speaks of creation, placed in the formula above gives the constant pi. The number of letters and number of words in John 1:1 in Greek, which is the New Testament verse which speaks of "the beginning", placed in the same formula gives the constant e. Let this sink in. This is not coincidental, but intentionally designed by God. It was not designed by Moses and John, the human writers of Genesis 1:1 and John 1:1, who wrote thousands of years apart in two different languages and didn't even know anything about mathematical constants pi and e. It was designed by God who inspired these writers to write each word and each letter exactly as they wrote it for the purpose of God revealing the truth of His Word to us, to you—the reader.

The mathematical constant "e" was originally discovered by the Swiss mathematician, Jacob Bernoulli in the 1600's and marked by the letter "e" in honor of Leonhard Euler in the 1700's.[3] Like pi, it is an irrational number and goes on for infinity beyond the decimal point. It is used to express compound interest and natural growth mathematically. The human author of John 1:1 could not have possibly known anything about the mathematical constant e. It is irrational to think that it is by mere chance coincidence that John 1:1 gives "e" as the result of the above equation and Genesis 1:1 gives "pi" by the same equation. Both verses talk about creation in the beginning. It must be intelligently designed into the written sentence by our Creator.

To summarize the mathematical phenomena in John 1:1,

- All words add up to 3627 = **39 x 93** (another reflective pair similar to 37 x 73).

- The 2nd and 3rd words, 719 + 58 = **777.**

- The 1st, 3rd, 4th, 7th, 9th, 12th, 13th, 14th, 15th, 16th words, 55+58+70+70+58+134+31+284+58+70 = **888.**

- The 1st, 4th, 5th, 7th, 8th, 9th words: 55+70+373+70+373+58 = **999.**

- The 1st, 4th, 5th, 15th, 16th, 17th words: 55 +70+373+58+70+373 = **999.**

- Adding the gematria of Gen 1:1 and John 1:1 = 2701 + 3627 = 6328, which is the 112th triangular number.

- Putting the number equivalents for the letters and the words in the same mathematical formula as previously shown in Genesis 1:1 yields the constant "e".

The mathematical phenomena in Genesis 1:1 and John 1:1 is not something that can be found in every single verse of the Bible, or in any written sentence. Most sentences do not have any kind of mathematical or numerical pattern. But these two verses have significant similar mathematical phenomena that are not in any way commonplace. It is actually quite extraordinary.

I understand that some people have little problem accepting Genesis 1:1 as being inspired from God, but discard the New Testament as being from God. And vice-versa, some believe the New Testament is inspired by God, and the Old Testament is no longer relevant. However, the mathematical links between Genesis 1:1 and John 1:1 show the inspiration and relevance of both the Old and New Testaments.

But there is much more to share. Make sure you are wide awake before starting to read the next chapter. It requires some concentration to follow. But I want to show you, amazingly, the connection between Genesis 1:1 and John 1:1 is much more than a mathematical phenomenon. There is mathematical linkage as well with these verses and the chemical makeup of all living things.

CHAPTER 4

DNA Link

Incredibly, there is more linkage between Genesis 1:1 and John 1:1 and creation. The numerical values that come out of Genesis 1:1 and John 1:1 are also linked to the numerical genetic coding in the DNA of all living organisms. I first learned of this phenomenon from a video on YouTube by Peter Bluer.[1] He based this video from the work of Vladimir shCherbak who published his research showing numerical codes in DNA. Vladimir shCherbak did not have any clue that his finding had any linkage to verses in the Bible, however it does.

It's a little complicated, but I will try to keep it simple and describe step by step how numbers in the molecular structure of the DNA of all living things link to the numbers of Genesis 1:1 and John 1:1. What I will show you in this chapter and chapters to come originates from Peter Bluer's work, but I have built on his work. I have come up with a "Proton Matrix", "Neutron Matrix" and "Nucleon Matrix" of numbers, representing the DNA of all living things that compares to scripture—initially Genesis 1:1 and John 1:1, but these verses are just the very tip of the iceberg.

Geek alert: If you are not interested in the specifics of how I came up with the numbers from DNA that make up the "Proton Matrix", "Neutron Matrix" and "Nucleon Matrix", you can skip the remainder of this section to the portion labeled "Correlation of Numbers from DNA with Scripture".

DNA (deoxyribonucleic acid) is the material in cells that contains the genetic information that defines all known living organisms. The building blocks for DNA are molecules called nucleobases. The four nucleobases are Adenine (A), Guanine (G), Thymine (T), and Cytosine (C). These four nucleobases are used to express the genetic code of all organisms and can be expressed in a simple table with 64 entries. Each entry is made up of a nucleotide triplet called a codon. Table 1 below shows how these codons can be expressed.

		A	G	T	C	
		AAA	AGA	ATA	ACA	A
	A	AAG	AGG	ATG	ACG	G
		AAT	AGT	ATT	ACT	T
		AAC	AGC	ATC	ACC	C
		GAA	GGA	GTA	GCA	A
	G	GAG	GGG	GTG	GCG	G
		GAT	GGT	GTT	GCT	T
		GAC	GGC	GTC	GCC	C
		TAA	TGA	TTA	TCA	A
	T	TAG	TGG	TTG	TCG	G
		TAT	TGT	TTT	TCT	T
		TAC	TGC	TTC	TCC	C
		CAA	CGA	CTA	CCA	A
	C	CAG	CGG	CTG	CCG	G
		CAT	CGT	CTT	CCT	T
		CAC	CGC	CTC	CCC	C

These nucleotide codons code to one of 20 amino acids that are found in the standard genetic code of all living things. In alphabetical order, these 20 amino acids are: Alanine (Ala), Arginine (Arg), Asparagine (Asn), Aspartic acid (Asp), Cysteine (Cys), Glutamine (Gln), Glutamic acid (Glu), Glycine (Gly), Histidine (His), Isoleucine (Ile), Leucine (Leu), Lysine (Lys), Methionine (Met), Phenylalanine (Phe), Proline (Pro), Serine (Ser), Threonine (Thr), Tryptophan (Trp), Tyrosine (Tyr), and Valine (Val). The triplet codon cube can then be expressed with the amino acids that code to each codon, as shown in Table 2.

Table 2. DNA Codons with Associated Amino Acid

		A		G		T		C		
A	AAA	Lys	AGA	Arg	ATA	Ile	ACA	Thr	A
	AAG	Lys	AGG	Arg	ATG	Met	ACG	Thr	G
	AAT	Asn	AGT	Ser	ATT	Ile	ACT	Thr	T
	AAC	Asn	AGC	Ser	ATC	Ile	ACC	Thr	C
G	GAA	Glu	GGA	Gly	GTA	Val	GCA	Ala	A
	GAG	Glu	GGG	Gly	GTG	Val	GCG	Ala	G
	GAT	Asp	GGT	Gly	GTT	Val	GCT	Ala	T
	GAC	Asp	GGC	Gly	GTC	Val	GCC	Ala	C
T	TAA	STOP	TGA	STOP	TTA	Leu	TCA	Ser	A
	TAG	STOP	TGG	Trp	TTG	Leu	TCG	Ser	G
	TAT	Tyr	TGT	Cys	TTT	Phe	TCT	Ser	T
	TAC	Tyr	TGC	Cys	TTC	Phe	TCC	Ser	C
C	CAA	Gln	CGA	Arg	CTA	Leu	CCA	Pro	A
	CAG	Gln	CGG	Arg	CTG	Leu	CCG	Pro	G
	CAT	His	CGT	Arg	CTT	Leu	CCT	Pro	T
	CAC	His	CGC	Arg	CTC	Leu	CCC	Pro	C

Each of these 20 amino acids has a molecular formula, as shown in Table 3 below, consisting of carbon, hydrogen, nitrogen, oxygen and in two cases sulfur.

Table 3. Molecular Formula of 20 Amino Acids Common in DNA

Amino Acid	3-letter Code	Molecular Formula
Alanine	Ala	$C_3H_7NO_2$
Arginine	Arg	$C_6H_{14}N_4O_2$
Asparagine	Asn	$C_4H_8N_2O_3$
Aspartic acid	Asp	$C_4H_7NO_4$
Cysteine	Cys	$C_3H_7NO_2S$
Glutamine	Gln	$C_5H_{10}N_2O_3$
Glutamic acid	Glu	$C_5H_9NO_4$
Glycine	Gly	$C_2H_5NO_2$
Histidine	His	$C_6H_9N_3O_2$
Isoleucine	Ile	$C_6H_{13}NO_2$
Leucine	Leu	$C_6H_{13}NO_2$
Lysine	Lys	$C_6H_{14}N_2O_2$
Methionine	Met	$C_5H_{11}NO_2S$
Phenylalanine	Phe	$C_9H_{11}NO_2$
Proline	Pro	$C_5H_9NO_2$
Serine	Ser	$C_3H_7NO_3$
Threonine	Thr	$C_4H_9NO_3$
Tryptophan	Trp	$C_{11}H_{12}N_2O_2$
Tyrosine	Tyr	$C_9H_{11}NO_3$
Valine	Val	$C_5H_{11}NO_2$

The specific molecular formula of each amino acid can be broken down into the number of protons and neutrons of each amino acid molecule. The atomic number of an element is equal to the number of protons found in the nucleus of every atom of that element. The atomic mass is equal to the number of protons plus the number of neutrons in the nucleus of every atom of that element. So, on the Periodic Table of Elements, Carbon (C) has an atomic number of 6 and an atomic mass of 12.011 amu (atomic mass units). This means that Carbon is made up of 6 protons and 6 neutrons (12.011-6 rounds to 6) in its nucleus. Each Hydrogen atom is made up of 1 proton (no neutrons, since the atomic mass of hydrogen is 1.008 amu). Each Nitrogen atom is made up of 7 protons and 7 neutrons, each Oxygen atom is made up of 8 protons and 8 neutrons, and each Sulfur atom is made up of 16 protons and 16 neutrons.

With this information you can determine the number of protons and the number of neutrons of each molecule of each of the amino acids. In Table 4 below, I show the number of protons, the number of neutrons and the number of nucleons, which is the number of protons plus neutrons, for each amino acid.

Table 4

Number of Protons, Neutrons and Nucleons in each Amino Acid Molecule

Amino Acid	3-letter Code	Molecular Formula	Total # Protons	Total # Neutrons	Total # Nucleons
Alanine	Ala	$C_3H_7NO_2$	48	41	89
Arginine	Arg	$C_6H_{14}N_4O_2$	94	80	174
Asparagine	Asn	$C_4H_8N_2O_3$	70	62	132
Aspartic acid	Asp	$C_4H_7NO_4$	70	63	133
Cysteine	Cys	$C_3H_7NO_2S$	64	57	121
Glutamine	Gln	$C_5H_{10}N_2O_3$	78	68	146
Glutamic acid	Glu	$C_5H_9NO_4$	78	69	147
Glycine	Gly	$C_2H_5NO_2$	40	35	75
Histidine	His	$C_6H_9N_3O_2$	82	73	155
Isoleucine	Ile	$C_6H_{13}NO_2$	72	59	131
Leucine	Leu	$C_6H_{13}NO_2$	72	59	131
Lysine	Lys	$C_6H_{14}N_2O_2$	80	66	146
Methionine	Met	$C_5H_{11}NO_2S$	80	69	149
Phenylalanine	Phe	$C_9H_{11}NO_2$	88	77	165
Proline	Pro	$C_5H_9NO_2$	62	53	115
Serine	Ser	$C_3H_7NO_3$	56	49	105
Threonine	Thr	$C_4H_9NO_3$	64	55	119
Tryptophan	Trp	$C_{11}H_{12}N_2O_2$	108	96	204
Tyrosine	Tyr	$C_9H_{11}NO_3$	96	85	181
Valine	Val	$C_5H_{11}NO_2$	64	53	117

As an example, the molecular formula of Alanine is $C_3H_7NO_2$. So, in each molecule of Alanine there are:

- 18 protons in Carbon (C), since the atomic number of C is 6 and there are 3 atoms of C in Alanine,

- 7 protons in Hydrogen (H), since the atomic number of H is 1 and there are 7 atoms of H in Alanine,

- 7 protons in Nitrogen (N), since the atomic number of N is 7 and there is 1 atom of N in Alanine,

- 16 protons in Oxygen (O) since the atomic number of O is 8 and there are 2 atoms of O in Alanine.

All together there are 18+7+7+16 = 48 protons in Alanine. Similarly, the number of neutrons can be determined, since there are 6 neutrons in carbon, 0 neutrons in hydrogen, 7 neutrons in nitrogen and 8 neutrons in oxygen. The number of nucleons is simply the number of protons and neutrons. The entire table of amino acids can then be determined as numbers representing the number of protons, neutrons and nucleons. These numbers can then be placed in what I will call the "Codon-Amino Acid Matrix" to make a Proton Matrix, a Neutron Matrix and a Nucleon Matrix. I will start with the Nucleon Matrix in Figure 1. The Nucleon Matrix is made up of the Codons and associated Amino Acids of Table 2 and the nucleon count (protons plus neutrons) of each molecule of the amino acids from Table 4.

Nucleon Matrix:

		A		G		T		C		
A	^{1}Lys	146	^{2}Arg	174	^{3}Ile	131	^{4}Thr	119	A	
	Lys	146	Arg	174	Met	149	Thr	119	G	
	Asn	132	Ser	105	Ile	131	Thr	119	T	
	Asn	132	Ser	105	Ile	131	Thr	119	C	
G	^{5}Glu	147	^{6}Gly	75	^{7}Val	117	^{8}Ala	89	A	
	Glu	147	Gly	75	Val	117	Ala	89	G	
	Asp	133	Gly	75	Val	117	Ala	89	T	
	Asp	133	Gly	75	Val	117	Ala	89	C	
T	^{9}STOP	0	^{10}STOP	0	^{11}Leu	131	^{12}Ser	105	A	
	STOP	0	Trp	204	Leu	131	Ser	105	G	
	Tyr	181	Cys	121	Phe	165	Ser	105	T	
	Tyr	181	Cys	121	Phe	165	Ser	105	C	
C	^{13}Gln	146	^{14}Arg	174	^{15}Leu	131	^{16}Pro	115	A	
	Gln	146	Arg	174	Leu	131	Pro	115	G	
	His	155	Arg	174	Leu	131	Pro	115	T	
	His	155	Arg	174	Leu	131	Pro	115	C	

556	558	542	476
560	300	468	356
362	446	592	420
602	696	524	460

Figure 1. Nucleon matrix of 16 numbers derived from the codons of Table 1, the associated amino acids of Table 2, and the nucleon count of Table 4.

Block 1 is the upper left block and is made up of two codons that code to Lysine (Lys) and two codons that code to Asparagine (Asn). If you add up the number of nucleons (the number of protons and neutrons) in two molecules of Lys (146+146) and two molecules of Asn (132+132), you get 556. So, block 1, the upper left block is 556. If you do the same for all blocks you get a Nucleon Matrix of 16 numbers shown in Figure 1.

Correlation of Numbers from DNA with Scripture

Now, I'd like to show how these numbers correlate to Genesis 1:1 *"In the beginning God created the heavens and the earth."* In Hebrew, with the corresponding numbers of each Hebrew word, Figure 2 below shows the corresponding phrases in Genesis 1:1 and the equivalent numbers in the Nucleon Matrix:

Nucleon Matrix				Genesis 1:1
556	558	542	476	296 407 395 401 86 203 913
560	300	468	356	בראשית ברא אלהים את השמים ואת הארץ:
362	446	592	420	913+203+86+395+407+296 = **2300** from Genesis 1:1
602	696	524	460	602+560+420+362+356 = **2300** from Nucleon Matrix

913+203+86+395+407+296 = **2300** from Genesis 1:1
602+560+420+362+356 = **2300** from Nucleon Matrix

203+86+401+395+407 = **1492** from Genesis 1:1
556 + 476 + 460 = **1492** from Nucleon Matrix

Figure 2. Correlation of Genesis 1:1 Gematria with the Nucleon Matrix derived from the 20 common amino acids of DNA.

The total gematria of Genesis 1:1 is 2701, and the Nucleon Matrix has only even numbers. So, you can't find the number "2701" in the Nucleon Matrix. But if you combine words together that make even numbers, you can see the connection. The first three words and last three words of Genesis 1:1 add up to 2300. The numbers in the Nucleon Matrix that add up to 2300 are underlined with a solid line (560+300+362+420+602). The second through sixth words of Genesis 1:1 add up to 1492. The Nucleon Matrix numbers 556, 476 and 460, underlined with a dashed line, add up to 1492.

There are more combinations of numbers in the Nucleon Matrix that add up to 2300, though. There are seven unique combinations of numbers in the Nucleon Matrix that add up to 2300. Starting with the largest number, the seven combinations are:

1) 696 + 602 + 556 + 446 = 2300

2) 696 + 602 + 542 + 460 = 2300

3) 602 + 560 + 476 + 362 + 300 = 2300

4) 602 + 560 + 420 + 362 + 356 = 2300

5) 592 + 542 + 446 + 420 + 300 = 2300

6) 558 + 556 + 524 + 362 + 300 = 2300

7) 558 + 556 + 468 + 362 + 356 = 2300

These seven combinations of numbers from the Nucleon Matrix that add up to 2300 utilize every number of the Nucleon Matrix. Notice the list contains "seven" combinations of numbers, corresponding again to the pattern of sevens in Genesis 1:1 previously shown.

Likewise, in John 1:1, there is also a correlation between the numbers associated with John 1:1 and the Nucleon Matrix as shown in Figure 3:

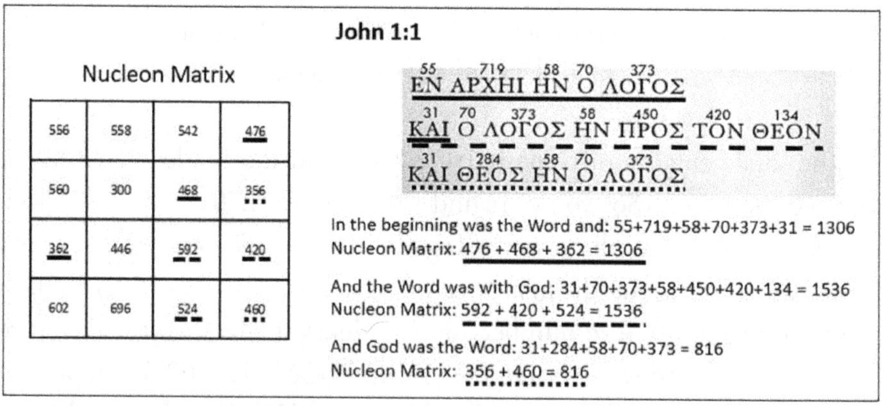

Figure 3. Correlation of John 1:1 Gematria with the Nucleon Matrix derived from the 20 common amino acids of DNA.

Thus, not only does Genesis 1:1 have gematria that links to the Nucleon Matrix, but John 1:1 does as well. Two different languages, two different human writers, who knew nothing about the DNA of all living things. You may think this could just be a coincidence, but now look at the connection if you add the gematria of Genesis 1:1 (2701) and the gematria of John 1:1 (3627) and compare to the DNA Nucleon Matrix as shown in Figure 4.

Nucleon Matrix				Genesis 1:1 and John 1:1
556	558	542	476	$2701 + 3627 = \mathbf{6328}$
560	300	468	356	
362	446	592	420	542 + 560 + 300 + 468 + 356 + 362 + 446 + 592 + 420 + 602 + 696 + 524 + 460 =
602	696	524	460	**6328**

Figure 4. Gematria of Genesis 1:1 plus gematria of John 1:1 correlation with the Nucleon Matrix

Thirteen of the sixteen numbers of the DNA Nucleon Matrix add up to 6328, the gematria of Genesis 1:1 and John 1:1. Another mere coincidence? To top it all off the three numbers that are not used from the Nucleon Matrix when adding Genesis 1:1 and John 1:1 together are 556, 558 and 476. The summation of these numbers is 1590. Two (and only two) incredible verses in the Old Testament have a gematria of 1590. One verse is Proverbs 30:6, *"Do not add to His words, or He will rebuke you and prove you a liar"*. The gematria of Proverbs 30:6 is 1590 as shown in Figure 5 below. The message of Proverbs 30:6 is: Do not add to His words. If you do then the math and DNA connections break.

Nucleon Matrix				
556	558	542	476
560	300	468	356
362	446	592	420
602	696	524	460

Proverbs 30:6

Do not add to His words, or He will rebuke you and prove you a liar.

אַל־תּוֹסְףְּ עַל־דְּבָרָיו פֶּן־יוֹכִיחַ בְּךָ וְנִכְזָבְתָּ׃

485   22   184   322   577

577+322+184+22+485 = **1590**

Nucleon Matrix: Blocks 1, 2 & 4 = 556+558+476 = **1590**

Figure 5. Correlation between Proverbs 30:6 and the DNA Nucleon Matrix

The other verse in the Old Testament with a gematria of 1590 is Psalm 66:5 which states *"Come and see what God has done, how awesome His works in man's behalf!"* Indeed, the puzzle pieces He has hidden in His word to connect Old and New Testament together and connect the DNA of all living things to His Word is extremely awesome. The connection of Psalm 66:5 with the Nucleon Matrix is shown in Figure 6.

Nucleon Matrix				
556	558	542	476
560	300	468	356
362	446	592	420
602	696	524	460

Psalms 66:5

Come and see what God has done, how awesome His works in man's behalf!

45   162   145   257   86   626   213   56

לְכוּ וּרְאוּ מִפְעֲלוֹת אֱלֹהִים נוֹרָא עֲלִילָה עַל־בְּנֵי אָדָם׃

56+213+626+86+257+145+162+45 = **1590**

Nucleon Matrix: Blocks 1, 2 & 4 = 556+558+476 = **1590**

Figure 6. Correlation between Psalms 66:5 and the DNA Nucleon Matrix.

What are the chances that the gematria of Genesis 1:1, John 1:1 and Proverbs 30:6 or Psalms 66:5 matching exactly with the Nucleon Matrix numbers? First, with a square of 16 numbers, there are 65,535 different number combinations when adding numbers together to get a unique combination. Appendix 3 shows in detail how this is derived. So, there is a 1 in 65,535 chance of getting a particular number sequence between 300, the smallest number in the Nucleon Matrix and 7918, the sum of all sixteen numbers. There are 22,098 verses in the Old Testament[2] and 7956 verses in the New Testament[3], for a total of 30,054 verses in the Bible. So, there is a 1 in 30,054 chance of selecting one of those verses. But if you had to randomly select three of those verses, there is a 1 in 4.52389×10^{12} chance of selecting those verses. Then to randomly connect those three verses to the Nucleon Matrix, multiplying 65,535 and 4.52389×10^{12} is a 1 in 2.96473×10^{17} chance of those three verses connecting to the Nucleon Matrix. It must have been designed to fit, not a random coincidence.

I will show many other verses in the Bible that have connections to the Nucleon Matrix in upcoming chapters. But before leaving Genesis 1:1 and John 1:1, I want to also show the connection of these verses with the Neutron Matrix and the Proton Matrix.

Neutron Matrix:

The Neutron Matrix also correlates to Genesis 1:1 and John 1:1. Taking the Codon-Amino acid Matrix and plugging in only the number of neutrons, gives a "Neutron Matrix" shown in Figure 7.

		A		G		T		C							
A	Lys	66	Arg	80	Ile	59	Thr	55	A		256	258	246	220
	Lys	66	Arg	80	Met	69	Thr	55	G					
	Asn	62	Ser	49	Ile	59	Thr	55	T					
	Asn	62	Ser	49	Ile	59	Thr	55	C					
G	Glu	69	Gly	35	Val	53	Ala	41	A		264	140	212	164
	Glu	69	Gly	35	Val	53	Ala	41	G					
	Asp	63	Gly	35	Val	53	Ala	41	T					
	Asp	63	Gly	35	Val	53	Ala	41	C					
T	STOP		STOP		Leu	59	Ser	49	A		170	210	272	196
	STOP		Trp	96	Leu	59	Ser	49	G					
	Tyr	85	Cys	57	Phe	77	Ser	49	T					
	Tyr	85	Cys	57	Phe	77	Ser	49	C					
C	Gln	68	Arg	80	Leu	59	Pro	53	A		282	320	236	212
	Gln	68	Arg	80	Leu	59	Pro	53	G					
	His	73	Arg	80	Leu	59	Pro	53	T					
	His	73	Arg	80	Leu	59	Pro	53	C					

Figure 7. Neutron matrix of 16 numbers derived from the codons of Table 1, the associated amino acids of Table 2, and the neutron count of Table 4.

In Figure 8 below, I show one correlation of numbers from the Neutron Matrix that add up to 2300 and one correlation of numbers from the

Neutron Matrix that add up to 1492 utilizing 15 of the 16 numbers in the Neutron Matrix.

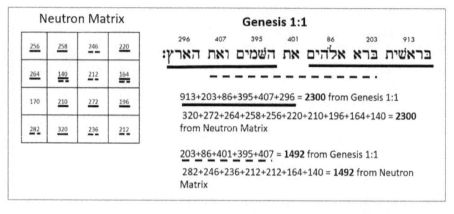

Figure 8. Correlation of Genesis 1:1 Gematria with the Neutron Matrix.

But there are actually 50 unique combinations of numbers that add up to 2300 from the Neutron Matrix and 65 unique combinations of numbers that add up to 1492 from the Neutron Matrix. Appendix 4 lists these combinations of numbers which link Genesis 1:1 to the Neutron Matrix. The linkage of the numbers derived from Genesis 1:1 and numbers derived from our DNA is solid.

Similarly, the Neutron Matrix correlates with John 1:1 as well, as shown in Figure 9 below.

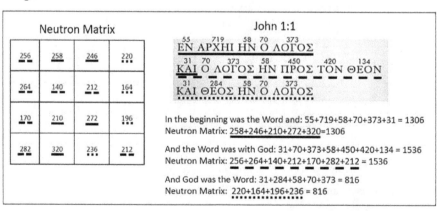

Figure 9. Correlation of John 1:1 Gematria with the Neutron Matrix derived from the 20 common amino acids of DNA.

In this case, every number of the Neutron Matrix is used one time to equate to the three phrases of John 1:1. But the Neutron Matrix has many other combinations of numbers than the ones shown in Figure 10 that correspond to John 1:1. Appendix 5 shows that there are 52 combinations of numbers from the Neutron Matrix that add up to 1306, the first phrase of John 1:1, 49 combinations of numbers that add up to 1536, the second phrase of John 1:1 and five combinations of numbers that add up to 816, the third phrase of John 1:1. I find this connection to be utterly amazing.

Proton Matrix

The Proton Matrix correlates to Genesis 1:1 and John 1:1 as well. Taking the Codon-Amino acid Matrix and plugging in only the number of protons, gives a "Proton Matrix" shown in Figure 10.

		A		G		T		C		
A	^{1}Lys	80	^{2}Arg	94	^{3}Ile	72	^{4}Thr	64	A
	Lys	80	Arg	94	Met	80	Thr	64	G
	Asn	70	Ser	56	Ile	72	Thr	64	T
	Asn	70	Ser	56	Ile	72	Thr	64	C
G	^{5}Glu	78	^{6}Gly	40	^{7}Val	64	^{8}Ala	48	A
	Glu	78	Gly	40	Val	64	Ala	48	G
	Asp	70	Gly	40	Val	64	Ala	48	T
	Asp	70	Gly	40	Val	64	Ala	48	C
T	^{9}STOP	0	^{10}STOP	0	^{11}Leu	72	^{12}Ser	56	A
	STOP	0	Trp	108	Leu	72	Ser	56	G
	Tyr	96	Cys	64	Phe	88	Ser	56	T
	Tyr	96	Cys	64	Phe	88	Ser	56	C
C	^{13}Gln	78	^{14}Arg	94	^{15}Leu	72	^{16}Pro	62	A
	Gln	78	Arg	94	Leu	72	Pro	62	G
	His	82	Arg	94	Leu	72	Pro	62	T
	His	82	Arg	94	Leu	72	Pro	62	C

300	300	296	256
296	160	256	192
192	236	320	224
320	376	288	248

Figure 10. Proton matrix of 16 numbers derived from the codons of Table 1, the associated amino acids of Table 2, and the proton count of Table 4.

The Proton Matrix correlates to Genesis 1:1 as shown in Figure 11. One combination of numbers is shown adding to 2300, the gematria of the first three and last three words of Genesis 1:1, and one combination of numbers is shown adding to 1492, the gematria of the second through sixth words.

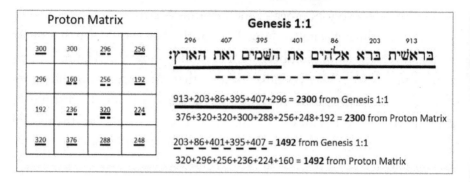

Figure 11. Correlation of Genesis 1:1 Gematria with the Proton
Matrix derived from the 20 common amino acids of DNA.

As in the case of the Nucleon and Neutron Matrices, there are many
more combinations of numbers that add to 2300 and 1492. Appendix 6
shows 33 combinations of numbers from the Proton Matrix that add to
2300 and 16 combinations of numbers from the Proton Matrix that add
to 1492 for a total of 49 (7 x 7) combinations of numbers from the Proton
Matrix that correlate to Genesis 1:1. The pattern of "sevens" in Genesis 1:1
comes out again in the correlation with the Proton Matrix.

To finish up, John 1:1 also correlates to the Proton Matrix as shown in
Figure 12. The first phrase and first two words of the second phrase add to
1376 and the numbers in the Proton Matrix underlined in a solid line add
to 1376. The second phrase of John 1:1 adds to 1536 and the numbers in
the Proton Matrix underlined in a dashed line add to 1536. And the third
phrase of John 1:1 adds to 816, and the numbers in the Proton Matrix that
are underlined with a dotted line add to 816.

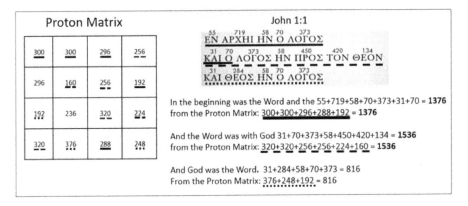

Figure 12. Correlation of John 1:1 Gematria with the Proton Matrix derived from the 20 common amino acids of DNA.

Likewise, there are many other numbers in the Proton Matrix that add up to the phrases of John 1:1. Appendix 7 shows 21 (3x7) combinations of numbers that add to 1376 and 29 combinations of numbers that add to 1536. In those 29 combinations, seven combinations start with the number 376, 14 combinations start with the number 320 and seven combinations start with the number 300, and then one last combination that starts with the number 296. There are two combinations of numbers from the Proton Matrix that add to 816, the one shown in Figure 12 and also 296+296+224=816.

So far, I've demonstrated that Genesis 1:1 and John 1:1 link together mathematically and link to the number of nucleons, neutrons and protons in the DNA codon matrices. God created the heavens and the earth and all life. He also inspired the Bible with mathematical and chemical connection to the words written in these two very important creation verses.

CHAPTER 5

Genesis 1:14

I've shown so far that Genesis 1:1 and John 1:1 link together and Genesis 1:1 has special mathematical properties originating from the gematria of the verse, 2701 which equals 37 x 73. Additionally, I've shown that these verses link to the proton and neutron numbers derived from the DNA of all living things. In this chapter I'm going to show how Genesis 1:14 links to the DNA numbers and Genesis 1:1. In English Genesis 1:14 says:

> *And God said, "Let there be lights in the expanse of the sky to separate the day from the night, and let them serve as signs to mark seasons and days and years..."*
>
> *— Genesis 1:14*

Figure 1 below shows Genesis 1:14 in Hebrew along with the numeric equivalent of each letter and the gematria (the sum of all letters in the word) for each word of the verse.

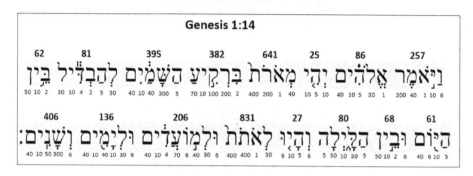

Figure 1. Genesis 1:14 in Hebrew with associated numbers and gematria for each word.

The gematria of Genesis 1:14 is 3744, all the words added together. The gematria of this verse has a solid connection with the Neutron Matrix and the Nucleon Matrix. First, I'd like to point out that the Neutron and Nucleon Matrices are each made up of 16 numbers. Genesis 1:14 contains 16 words, so we are comparing 16 numbers of the verse with 16 numbers of the Neutron and Nucleon Matrices. Figure 2 shows the Neutron Matrix. All of the numbers of the Neutron Matrix add to 3658. Fifteen of the sixteen words of Genesis 1:14 also add to 3658.

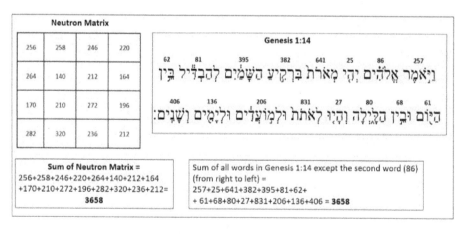

Figure 2. Correlation between Neutron Matrix and Genesis 1:14

Genesis 1:14 also has a solid connection also with the Nucleon Matrix. From the Nucleon Matrix there are 49 (7x7) unique combinations of numbers that add to 3744, the gematria of Genesis 1:14. Figure 3 shows three of those combinations utilizing every number of the Nucleon Matrix and Table 1 shows all 49 combinations.

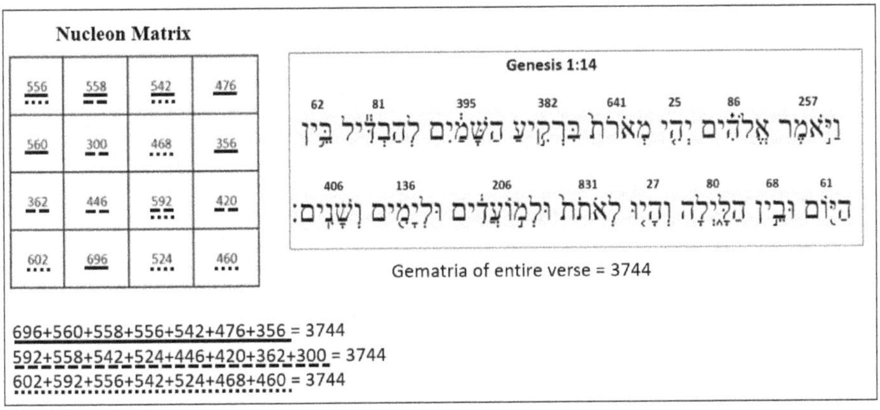

Figure 3. Correlation of Genesis 1:14 with Nucleon Matrix

Table 1. Correlation of Genesis 1:14 with the Nucleon Matrix

#																		
1	696	602	592			556			476		460			362			=	3744
2	696	602			558	556		524				446		362			=	3744
3	696	602			558		542	524			460			362			=	3744
4	696	602			558			524	476	468			420				=	3744
5	696	602				556	542	524		468					354		=	3744
6	696	602				556	542			468	460		420				=	3744
7	696		592	560	558	556							420	362			=	3744
8	696		592	560		556		524			460						=	3744
9	696		592	560			542	524		468				362			=	3744
10	696		592		558	556			476			446	420				=	3744
11	696		592		558		542	524	476					354			=	3744
12	696		592		558		542		476		460		420				=	3744
13	696		592		558			524		468	460	446					=	3744
14	696		592		558						460		420	362	354	300	=	3744
15	696		592				542	524	476	468		446					=	3744
16	696		592				542		476				420	362	354	300	=	3744
17	696		592					524		468		446	420	362	354	300	=	3744
18	696		592							468	460	446	420	362		300	=	3744
19	696			560	558	556	542		476						354		=	3744
20	696			560	558	556				468	460	446					=	3744
21	696			560		556	542	524				446	420				=	3744
22	696			560		556	542		476	468		446					=	3744
23	696			560		556				468		446		362	354	300	=	3744
24	696			560			542			468	460			362	354	300	=	3744
25	696						542	524			460	446	420		354	300	=	3744
26	696						542		476	468	460			362	354	300	=	3744
27		602	592	560						468		446	420				=	3744
28		602	592			556	542	524		468	460						=	3744
29		602	592					524	476	468			420	362		300	=	3744
30		602		560	558	556		524	476	468							=	3744
31		602		560					476	468			420		354	300	=	3744
32		602			558	556	542			468				362	354	300	=	3744
33		602			558			524	476	468	460				354	300	=	3744
34		602			558			524	476			446	420	362	354		=	3744
35		602				556	542		476		460	446		362		300	=	3744
36		602				556	542			468	460	446	420	362	354		=	3744
37			592	560	558	556	542		476		460						=	3744
38			592	560	558						460			362	354	300	=	3744
39			592	560		556	542		476					362	354	300	=	3744
40			592	560		556				468	460	446		362		300	=	3744
41			592		558	556			476		460	446			354	300	=	3744
42			592		558		542	524				446	420	362		300	=	3744
43			592		558		542		476	468		446		362		300	=	3744
44			592		558		542			468		446	420	362	354		=	3744
45				560	558	556	542					446	420	362		300	=	3744
46				560	558			524	476		460	446	420			300	=	3744
47				560	558				476	468	460	446	420		354		=	3744
48				560			558	542	524			460	446		354	300	=	3744
49					558		542	524	476	468	460			362	354		=	3744

It is significant that there are exactly 49 (7x7) unique combinations of numbers from the Nucleon Matrix that add to 3744, the gematria of Genesis 1:14. We recognized a pattern of "sevens" in Genesis 1:1. It is interesting enough to show linkage between the Nucleon Matrix and Genesis 1:14, but that there are 49 unique combinations is even more significant.

There is a much stronger connection between Genesis 1:1 and Genesis 1:14, though. An interesting numerical phenomenon about Genesis 1:14 is that various combinations of numbers of the words of this verse add to 111, 222, 333, 444, 555, 666, 777, 888, and 999. Placing the numbers corresponding to the words in Genesis 1:14 in sequential order from greatest to least enables easier viewing how the numbers associated with different words add up to the triple digit numbers. Table 2 shows all the combinations.

Table 2. Word/Number Combinations from Genesis 1:14

	831	641	406	395	382	257	206	136	86	81	80	68	62	61	27	25		
1									86							25	=	111
1								136	86								=	222
2								136						61		25	=	222
3										81	80			61			=	222
1									86	81	80			61		25	=	333
1					382								62				=	444
2							206			81		68	62		27		=	444
3								136	86	81	80			61			=	444
1			406							81		68					=	555
2					382				86				62			25	=	555
3					382						80	68				25	=	555
4							206	136		81	80				27	25	=	555
5							206		86	81		68	62		27	25	=	555
1		641														25	=	666
2			406						86	81		68				25	=	666
3				395							80	68	62	61			=	666
4					382	257									27		=	666
5					382			136	86				62				=	666
6					382			136			80	68					=	666
7					382			136					62	61		25	=	666
8					382					81	80		62	61			=	666
9							206	136	86	81		68	62		27		=	666
10							206	136		81		68	62	61	27	25	=	666
1		641						136									=	777
2			406			257							62		27	25	=	777
3			406					136	86	81		68					=	777
4			406					136		81		68		61		25	=	777
5				395	382												=	777
6				395			206			81		68			27		=	777
7				395					86		80	68	62	61		25	=	777
8					382	257			86						27	25	=	777
9					382			136	86		80	68				25	=	777
10					382				86	81	80		62	61		25	=	777

Table 2 continued on the next page.

Table 2 Continued

	831	641	406	395	382	257	206	136	86	81	80	68	62	61	27	25	=	
1		641						136	86							25	=	888
2		641							86	81	80						=	888
3		641								81	80			61		25	=	888
4			406	395									62			25	=	888
5			406			257		136					62		27		=	888
6				395	382				86							25	=	888
7				395		257			86				62	61	27		=	888
8				395		257				81		68	62			25	=	888
9				395		257					80	68		61	27		=	888
10				395			206		86	81		68			27	25	=	888
11				395				136	86		80	68	62	61			=	888
12					382	257		136	86						27		=	888
13					382	257		136						61	27	25	=	888
14					382	257				81	80			61	27		=	888
15					382			136	86	81	80		62	61			=	888
16						257	206	136	86		80		62	61			=	888
1	831									81			62			25	=	999
2	831										80			61	27			999
3		641						136		81	80			61			=	999
4		641							86	81		68	62	61			=	999
5			406	395				136					62				=	999
6			406		382					81		68	62				=	999
7			406			257	206					68	62				=	999
8			406			257		136	86				62		27	25	=	999
9			406			257		136			80	68			27	25	=	999
10			406			257			86	81	80		62		27		=	999
11			406			257				81	80		62	61	27	25	=	999
12				395	382			136	86								=	999
13				395	382			136						61		25	=	999
14				395	382					81	80			61			=	999
15				395		257	206				80			61			=	999
16				395		257		136		81		68	62				=	999
17				395		257			86		80	68		61	27	25	=	999
18				395			206	136	86	81		68			27		=	999
19				395			206	136		81		68		61	27	25	=	999
20				395			206	136			80	68	62		27	25	=	999
21					382	257	206		86			68					=	999
22					382	257	206					68		61		25	=	999
23					382	257			86	81	80			61	27	25	=	999
24					382		206	136		81	80		62		27	25	=	999

Derived from Genesis 1:14, there is one combination of numbers that add to 111 and 333, three combinations of numbers that add to 222 and 444, five combinations of numbers that add to 555, ten combinations of numbers that add to 666 and 777, sixteen combinations of numbers that add to 888 and twenty-four combinations of numbers that add to 999. Connecting to Geneses 1:1, there are **37** combinations of numbers that add to 111, 222, 333, 444, 555 and 999 and there are **73** combinations of numbers in total that add to 111, 222, 333, 444, 555, 666 ,777, 888, and 999.

The verse states that the lights in the sky will serve as *signs* to mark seasons and days and years. The 37 and 73 hidden in Genesis 1:14 is an intentional design (sign) of this scripture linking it to Genesis 1:1, that God created the heavens. Genesis 1:1 also has 777, 888 and 999 from various words added together.

The God who created the heavens and the earth, also inspired the verses about His creation with numerical patterns in the words that reveal intelligent mathematical design.

CHAPTER 6

Created in the image of God

In the account of creation in Genesis Chapter 1, the last and greatest thing that God created was human beings, created in His own image. God created human beings, male and female with a physical body, a soul and a spirit. The physical aspects of human beings and animals are a masterpiece of creation. However, we are much more than physical beings. The soul of each individual is where we get thoughts, feelings, personality. And with the spiritual aspect of being created in the image of God, we have the capacity to interact with God through our spirit. The key verse where God writes about the creation of mankind is:

> *So God created man in His own image.*
> *In the image of God He created him,*
> *Male and female He created them.*
>
> *– Genesis 1:27*

In Hebrew, Genesis 1:27 has the symmetry of four words in the first phrase, four words in the second phrase and four words in the third phrase as shown in Figure 1 below. The first phrase has 21 letters, a multiple of seven. The second phrase has 15 letters, a multiple of five, and the third phrase has 14 letters, a multiple of seven. The gematria of Genesis 1:27 is 2816

(219 + 86 + 451 + 168 + 162 + 86 + 203 + 407 + 227 + 163 + 203 + 441 = 2816).

Number of Words	Number of Letters	Genesis 1:27	
4	21 (3x7)	וַיִּבְרָ֨א אֱלֹהִ֤ים ׀ אֶת־הָֽאָדָם֙ בְּצַלְמ֔וֹ 168 451 86 219	And created God the man in His image;
4	15 (3x5)	בְּצֶ֥לֶם אֱלֹהִ֖ים בָּרָ֣א אֹת֑וֹ 407 203 86 162	in the image of God created him,
4	14 (2x7)	זָכָ֥ר וּנְקֵבָ֖ה בָּרָ֥א אֹתָֽם׃ 441 203 163 227	male and female created them.

Gematria of entire verse is 2816.

Figure 1. Structure and Gematria of Genesis 1:27.

The number, 2816 is interesting with a prime factorization of 2^8 x 11. Other ways of factorizing 2816 are:

2816 =

22 x 8 x 8 x 2

44 x 8 x 8

88 x 4 x 4 x 2

The symmetry of the factors of 2816 is "two": 2 digits that are the same multiplied by 2 other digits that are the same and in two cases above multiplied by 2. This connects with the "male" and "female" aspect of God's creation of mankind in His image.

The gematria of Genesis 1:27 has a solid connection numerically with the Nucleon Matrix, Proton Matrix and Neutron Matrix that I introduced in Chapter 4. This connection links the proton and neutron counts of the molecules of the main amino acids in the DNA of all living things to this verse about the creation of mankind. There are 24 different combinations of numbers in the Nucleon Matrix that add to 2816. Three of those combinations are shown in Figure 2 and all 24 are listed in Appendix 8.

	Nucleon Matrix			Genesis 1:27	

Nucleon Matrix **Genesis 1:27**

556	558	542	476
560	300	468	356
362	446	592	420
602	696	524	460

וַיִּבְרָ֨א אֱלֹהִ֤ים ׀ אֶת־הָֽאָדָם֙ בְּצַלְמ֔וֹ   And created God the man in His image;
168   451   86   219

בְּצֶ֥לֶם אֱלֹהִ֖ים בָּרָ֣א אֹת֑וֹ   in the image of God created him,
407   203   86   162

זָכָ֥ר וּנְקֵבָ֖ה בָּרָ֥א אֹתָֽם׃   male and female created them.
441   203   163   227

696+558+460+446+356+300=2816
602+592+556+542+524 = 2816
592+560+476+468+420+300=2816

Gematria of Genesis 1:27 = 2816
168+451+86+219+407+203+86+162+441+203+163+227 = 2816

Figure 2. Three combinations of numbers from Nucleon
Matrix that equal gematria of Genesis 1:27

There are also 24 different combinations of numbers from the Proton Matrix that add up to 2816, the gematria of Genesis 1:27. Two of those combinations of numbers are shown in Figure 3 and all 24 combinations are listed in Appendix 8.

Proton Matrix **Genesis 1:27**

300	300	296	256
296	160	256	192
192	236	320	224
320	376	288	248

וַיִּבְרָ֨א אֱלֹהִ֤ים ׀ אֶת־הָֽאָדָם֙ בְּצַלְמ֔וֹ   And created God the man in His image;
168   451   86   219

בְּצֶ֥לֶם אֱלֹהִ֖ים בָּרָ֣א אֹת֑וֹ   in the image of God created him,
407   203   86   162

זָכָ֥ר וּנְקֵבָ֖ה בָּרָ֥א אֹתָֽם׃   male and female created them.
441   203   163   227

376+300+296+296+288+256+236
+224+192+192+160=**2816**

320+320+300+296+288+256
+256+248+236=**2816**

Gematria of Genesis 1:27 = **2816**

168+451+86+219+407+203+86+
162+441+203+163+227 = **2816**

Figure 3. Two combinations of numbers from the
Proton Matrix that equal the gematria of Genesis 1:27

Lastly, there are 13 different combinations of numbers from the Neutron Matrix that add up to 2816, all listed in Appendix 8. Twelve of the combinations have 12 numbers that add up to 2816 and one sequence, shown in Figure 4 has 13 numbers that add up to 2816.

Neutron Matrix				Genesis 1:27	
256	258	246	220	וַיִּבְרָא אֱלֹהִים ׀ אֶת־הָאָדָם בְּצַלְמֹו	And created God the man in His image;
				168 451 86 219	
264	140	212	164	בְּצֶלֶם אֱלֹהִים בָּרָא אֹתֹו	in the image of God created him,
				407 203 86 162	
170	210	272	196	זָכָר וּנְקֵבָה בָּרָא אֹתָם:	male and female created them.
				441 203 163 227	
282	320	236	212		

282+272+256+246+236+220+212
+210+196+170+164+140 = **2816**

Gematria of Genesis 1:27 = **2816**

168+451+86+219+407+203+86+
162+441+203+163+227 = **2816**

Figure 4. One set of numbers from the Neutron Matrix with sum of 2816, the gematria of Genesis 1:27

So far I've shown the combinations of numbers in the Nucleon, Proton and Neutron matrices that sum to 2816, the gematria of Genesis 1:27. If you split apart the three phrases of Genesis 1:27, there are many more connections with the Neutron Matrix. The gematria of the three phrases of Genesis 1:27 is shown in Figure 5.

Genesis 1:27

168+451+86+219 = **924**	וַיִּבְרָא אֱלֹהִים ׀ אֶת־הָאָדָם בְּצַלְמֹו 168 451 86 219	And created God the man in His image;
407+203+86+162 = **858**	בְּצֶלֶם אֱלֹהִים בָּרָא אֹתֹו 407 203 86 162	in the image of God created him,
441+203+163+227 = **1034**	זָכָר וּנְקֵבָה בָּרָא אֹתָם: 441 203 163 227	male and female created them.

Gematria of entire verse is 2816.

Figure 5. Gematria of each phrase of Genesis 1:27.

The gematria of the first phrase *"And created God the man in His image"* is 924. In the equation, 924 = 77 x 12, notice two digits of seven. Seven is a representation of God—spiritual completeness and perfection. And I believe two sevens, making up the number 77, can be a representation of man (male and female) in the image of God. Twelve is symbolic of the governing authority of man, with the 12 Tribes of Israel, 12 Apostles, 12 months in a year, 24 (12 x 2) hours in a day.

In the Neutron Matrix, there are 13 different combination of numbers that add to 924. Twelve of the combinations are made up of four different numbers, and one combination is made up of five numbers. The thirteen combinations adding to 924 are shown in Figure 6, with the combination of five numbers underlined in the Neutron Matrix.

Genesis 1:27 First Phrase			
Neutron Matrix			
256	258	246	220
264	140	212	164
170	210	272	196
282	320	236	212

וַיִּבְרָא אֱלֹהִים | אֶת־הָאָדָם בְּצַלְמוֹ   And created God the man in His image;

168   451   86   219

168+451+86+219 = **924**

140+164+196+212+212 = 924
140+246+256+282 = 924
164+220+258+282 = 924
164+246+256+258 = 924
170+236+246+272 = 924
196+210+236+282 = 924
196+210+246+272 = 924
196+220+236+272 = 924

210+212+220+282 = 924
210+212+246+256 = 924
210+220+236+258 = 924
212+212+236+264 = 924
212+220+236+256 = 924

Figure 6. Numbers from the Neutron Matrix that equal the gematria of the first phrase of Genesis 1:27.

The gematria of the second phrase of Genesis 1:27 *"in the image of God created him"* is 858. In the equation, 858 = 26 x 33, notice again, two digits, this time two 3's, making up 33. The number, 3, is a representation of the triune God, and two 3's can be a representation of man (male and female) in the image of God. Also, the number 26 is the gematria of LORD. In the Neutron Matrix there are 12 combinations of numbers that add up to 858 using every number of the Neutron Matrix. Figure 7 shows these combinations.

Genesis 1:27 Second Phrase

Neutron Matrix			
256	258	246	220
264	140	212	164
170	210	272	196
282	320	236	212

בְּצֶלֶם אֱלֹהִים בָּרָא אֹתוֹ   in the image of God created him,

407   203   86   162

407+203+86+162 = 858

140+164+272+282 = 858   170+196+220+272 = 858
140+210+236+272 = 858   170+196+236+256 = 858
140+196+258+264 = 858   170+210+220+258 = 858
164+210+220+264 = 858   170+212+212+264 = 858
164+212+236+246 = 858   170+212+220+256 = 858
170+196+210+282 = 858   256+282+320 = 858

Figure 7. Number sets from the Neutron Matrix that sum to 858, the gematria of the second phrase of Genesis 1:27.

Before moving on, I'd like to expand on the gematria of LORD and my reference to the "triune" God. The first primary number representing God is the number one. Deuteronomy 6:4 states *"Hear O Israel, the LORD our God the LORD is one."* One of the foundations of Christian doctrine is that the LORD is one, but is triune in nature: Father, Son and Holy Spirit. The first letter of the Hebrew alphabet, the Aleph, is a good symbol to demonstrate the "triune God" as ONE. The Aleph pictured below is the first letter of the Hebrew alphabet and represents the number 1.

If you notice it is made up of three strokes, a leaning Vav ו , and two Yods י . The numerical equivalent of the Hebrew letter Vav is six, and the numerical equivalent of the Hebrew letter Yod is ten. Adding them all up gives 6+10+10 = 26. Similarly, the gematria of the Tetragrammaton (LORD) in the Old Testament is 26.

5   6   5   10

The Yod is ten, the Hei is five, the Vav is six and the second Hei is five. Adding them all up gives 10+5+6+5 = 26. The Lord is ONE. It is possible to have ONE God with three forms: Father, Son and Holy Spirit. Three characteristics of God are His omniscience, omnipresence and omnipotence. The angels in Revelation 4:8 never stop saying, "*Holy, holy, holy is the Lord God Almighty, who was, and is, and is to come.*" Three times "holy", to the Eternal God past, present and future. So, the number one can represent God, the number three can represent God, and the number 26 can represent God, the LORD.

Lastly, the gematria of the third phrase of Genesis 1:27, "*male and female created them*" is 1034. In the equation 1034 = 47 x 22, the double digit of two again corresponds to male and female. The Neutron Matrix contains 18 unique combinations of numbers from the Neutron Matrix that add up to 1034. The first occurrence of each number in the sequence adding to 1034 is underlined in the number sequences and in the Neutron Matrix in Figure 8.

Neutron Matrix					
256	258	246	220	196+236+282+320 = 1034	140+164+220+246+264 = 1034
				196+246+272+320 = 1034	140+170+196+246+282 = 1034
				210+246+258+320 = 1034	140+170+196+256+272 = 1034
264	140	212	164	212+220+282+320 = 1034	140+170+210+256+258 = 1034
				212+246+256+320 = 1034	140+170+220+246+258 = 1034
170	210	272	196	220+236+258+320 = 1034	164+170+196+246+258 = 1034
				140+164+210+256+264 = 1034	164+210+212+212+236 = 1034
282	320	236	212	140+164+212+236+282 = 1034	170+196+210+212+246 = 1034
				140+164+212+246+272 = 1034	170+196+212+220+236 = 1034

Figure 8. Eighteen combinations of numbers from Neutron Matrix that add to 1034, the gematria of the third phrase of Genesis 1:27.

It's not just that one combination of numbers in the Neutron Matrix add up to the gematria of each phrase in Genesis 1:27, but multiple combination of numbers. It makes the connection even more solid.

One of the phenomena of Genesis 1:1 and John 1:1 is the numbers 777, 888 and 999 (twice) are found from adding some of the words of those verses. The numbers 777, 888 and 999 twice can be derived from Genesis

1:27, as well. The number strings that make up 777, 888 and 999 are below in Figure 9.

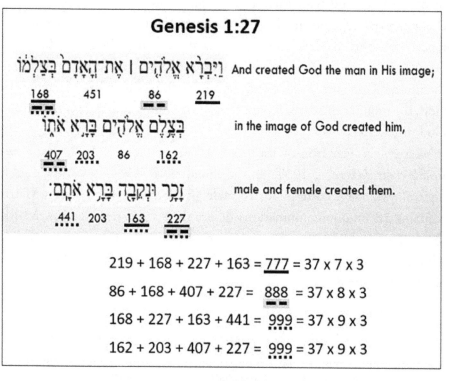

Figure 9. Words from Genesis 1:27 that add to 777, 888 and 999 twice.

Genesis 1:27 is a packed verse. It has

- Numerical symmetry in its structure: 4 x 4 x 4 words, first and last phrase multiple of seven and middle phrase multiple of five.

- Numerical symmetry in its gematria: 2816 = 44 x 8 x 8 or 22 x 8 x 8 x 2 or 88 x 4 x 4 x 2, with the predominance of two digits representing male and female.

- Multiple combinations of numbers from the Nucleon, Proton and Neutron Matrices add to 2816, which is the gematria of Genesis 1:27.

- The gematria of each phrase of Genesis 1:27 is found multiple times in the Neutron Matrix, in multiples of double digits.

- The special numbers of 777, 888 and 999, found in Genesis 1:1 and John 1:1 also occur in Gen 1:27.

Another key verse in Genesis concerning the creation of human beings, male and female, is Genesis 2:23. This verse expands that the woman was created from the man. This verse in Hebrew has symmetry with six words and 28 letters in the first major phrase and six words and 28 letters in the second major phrase (Figure 10). The gematria of these two phrases add to exactly 4000.

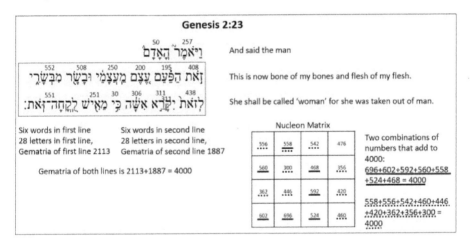

Figure 10. Connection between Genesis 2:23 and the Nucleon Matrix.

Two combinations of numbers from the Nucleon Matrix are shown to equal 4000 in Figure 10. There are actually 46 different combinations of numbers that add to 4000 from the Nucleon Matrix, as shown in Appendix 9. Forty-six is an interesting number because it is the number of chromosomes in a human being.

Are all of these numerical phenomena just some wild coincidence? All of these numerical connections between the gematria of Genesis 1:27 and the numbers of the Nucleon, Proton and Neutron Matrices, derived from the proton and neutron counts of the common amino acids in the DNA of all living things point to a common divinely inspired source. Genesis 2:23 further shows connection with our DNA and the number of chromosomes in human beings. We have a Creator, who created us in His image and the Creator gave us His Word to reveal Himself to us. He left his signature for discovery in the connection of these numbers by the human beings He created.

## CHAPTER 7

DNA Link to Key New Testament Verses

Moving on to the New Testament, I'd like to share some other key verses that have correlation with the Nucleon Matrix.

Colossians 1:17

First, Colossians 1:17 *"He is before all things, and in Him all things hold together."* Figure 1 below shows the Greek words of Colossians 1:17, word-for-word translation into English, and the number associated with each word. The total number of letters in Colossians 1:17 is 49 (7x7) and the gematria of the entire verse is 6666. In the Nucleon Matrix 14 out of the 16 numbers add up to 6666. Indeed, God created the universe and all living things, and he holds it all together, and he has hidden his design as a clue numerically in his Word and in the DNA of all living things.

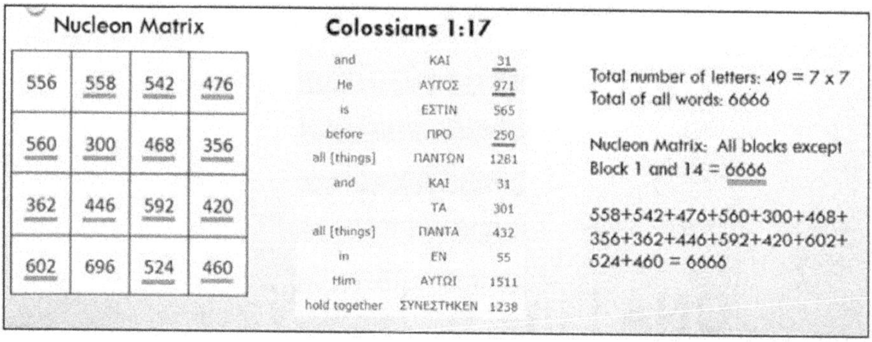

Figure 1. Correlation of Colossians 1:17 with the DNA Nucleon Matrix[1]

The two remaining blocks in the Nucleon Matrix that are not used in the numbers adding to 6666 are 556 and 696, not underlined in Figure 1. These numbers add to 1252. The numbers underlined in Colossians 1:17 in the figure above also add up to 1252 (31+971+250). Is it a coincidence that the message of this verse, that He is before all things and that in Him all things hold together, correlate to the DNA Nucleon Matrix by using each number in the matrix one time? It has to be an intentional design.

Matthew 5:18

There is a verse in the New Testament that talks about not removing a single letter from the Word of God. Jesus says in the Sermon on the Mount:

> *I tell you the truth, until heaven and earth disappear, not the smallest letter, not the least stroke of a pen, will by any means disappear from the Law until everything is accomplished.*
>
> *– Matthew 5:18*

The gematria of Matthew 5:18 is 9384, from 27 Greek words. The total of all numbers of the Nucleon Matrix is 7918. The number 7918 can be derived from Matthew 18 by using all the words except the first word, "truly" and the 12th-17th words (Figure 2).

Matthew 5:18

1	(for) truly	AMHN	99	99	
2		ГАР	104		104
3	I say	ΛЕГΩ	838		838
4	to you	YMIN	500		500
5	until	EΩΣ	1005		1005
6		AN	51		51
7	shall pass away	ПАРЕΛΘΗ	243		243
8	the	Ο	70		70
9	heaven	ΟΥΡΑΝΟΣ	891		891
10	and	KAI	31		31
11	the	H	8		8
12	earth	ГН	11	11	
13	iota	IΩTA	1111	1111	
14	one	EN	55	55	
15	or	H	8	8	
16	one	MIA	51	51	
17	stroke of a letter	ΚΕΡΕΑ	131	131	
18	no	ΟΥ	470		470
19	not	MH	48		48
20	shall pass away	ПАРЕΛΘΗ	243		243
21	from	AПO	151		151
22	the	ΤΟΥ	770		770
23	Law	NOMOY	630		630
24	until	EΩΣ	1005		1005
25	all	AN	51		51
26	all	ПАNTA	432		432
27	is accomplished	ГЕNHTAI	377		377
				1466	7918

Nucleon Matrix

556	558	542	476
560	300	468	356
362	446	592	420
602	696	524	460

Total of all numbers in the Nucleon Matrix is **7918**.

Figure 2. Correlation between Matthew 5:18 and the Nucleon Matrix

There are other ways to demonstrate a connection between Matthew 5:18 and the Nucleon Matrix by splitting up Matthew 5:18 into two parts. Figure 3 shows the phrase underlined *"until heaven and earth disappear, not the smallest letter, not the least stroke of a pen"* with a gematria of 3666. There are 35 (7x5) different combinations of numbers in the Nucleon Matrix that add up to 3666. Three of those combinations are shown in Figure 3. All 35 combinations of numbers from the Nucleon Matrix that add to 3666 are shown in Appendix 10.

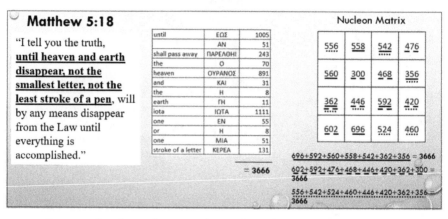

Matthew 5:18

"I tell you the truth, **until heaven and earth disappear, not the smallest letter, not the least stroke of a pen**, will by any means disappear from the Law until everything is accomplished."

until	ΕΩΣ	1005
	ΑΝ	51
shall pass away	ΠΑΡΕΛΘΗΙ	243
the	Ο	70
heaven	ΟΥΡΑΝΟΣ	891
and	ΚΑΙ	31
the	Η	8
earth	ΓΗ	11
iota	ΙΩΤΑ	1111
one	ΕΝ	55
or	Η	8
one	ΜΙΑ	51
stroke of a letter	ΚΕΡΕΑ	131

= **3666**

Nucleon Matrix

556	558	542	476
560	300	468	356
362	446	592	420
602	696	524	460

696+592+560+558+542+362+356 = **3666**

602+592+476+468+446+420+362+300 = **3666**

556+542+524+460+446+420+362+356 = **3666**

Figure 3. Correlation between phrase of Matthew 5:18 with Nucleon Matrix

The remaining words of this verse, "*I tell you the truth … will by any means disappear from the Law until everything is accomplished*" is shown in Greek in Figure 4 with a gematria of 5718. There are seven different combinations of numbers from the Nucleon Matrix that add to 5718, shown in Appendix 10. Two of those combinations are shown in Figure 4 utilizing every number of the Nucleon Matrix at least once.

Matthew 5:18

"**I tell you the truth**, until heaven and earth disappear, not the smallest letter, not the least stroke of a pen, **will by any means disappear from the Law until everything is accomplished**."

[for] truly	ΑΜΗΝ	99
	ΓΑΡ	104
I say	ΛΕΓΩ	838
to you	ΥΜΙΝ	500
no	ΟΥ	470
not	ΜΗ	48
shall pass away	ΠΑΡΕΛΘΗΙ	243
from	ΑΠΟ	151
the	ΤΟΥ	770
Law	ΝΟΜΟΥ	630
until	ΕΩΣ	1005
	ΑΝ	51
all	ΠΑΝΤΑ	432
is accomplished	ΓΕΝΗΤΑΙ	377

= **5718**

Nucleon Matrix

556	558	542	476
560	300	468	356
362	446	592	420
602	696	524	460

696+602+592+560+558+524+476+468+460+420+362 = **5718**

602+592+558+556+542+476+468+460+446+362+356+300 = **5718**

Figure 4. Correlation between phrase of Matthew 5:18 with Nucleon Matrix.

There are other ways to slice up Matthew 5:18 that connect with the Nucleon Matrix as well. The phrase "until heaven and earth disappear" has a gematria of 2310, and there are 12 different combination of numbers from the Nucleon Matrix that add up to 2310, shown in Appendix 10. Figure 5 shows three of those combinations.

Matthew 5:18				Nucleon Matrix			
"I tell you the truth,	until	ΕΩΣ	1005	556	558	542	476
until heaven and earth		AN	51				
disappear, not the	shall pass away	ΠΑΡΕΛΘΗ	243	560	300	468	356
smallest letter, not the	the	Ο	70				
least stroke of a pen, will	heaven	ΟΥΡΑΝΟΣ	891	362	446	592	420
by any means disappear	and	ΚΑΙ	31				
from the Law until	the	Η	8	602	696	524	460
everything is	earth	ΓΗ	11				
accomplished."			= 2310	696+476+420+362+356 = 2310			
				602+592+560+556 = 2310			
				558+524+468+460+300 = 2310			

Figure 5. Correlation between phrase of Matthew 5:18 with Nucleon Matrix.

The next phrase, *"not the smallest letter, not the least stroke of a pen"* has a gematria of 1356 in Greek. There are two combination of numbers from the DNA Nucleon Matrix that add up to 1356, shown in Figure 6.

Matthew 5:18				Nucleon Matrix			
"I tell you the truth,				556	558	542	476
until heaven and earth	iota	ΙΩΤΑ	1111				
disappear, **not the**	one	ΕΝ	55	560	300	468	356
smallest letter, not the	or	Η	8				
least stroke of a pen, will	one	ΜΙΑ	51	362	446	592	420
by any means disappear	stroke of a letter	ΚΕΡΕΑ	131				
from the Law until			= 1356	602	696	524	460
everything is				524+476+356 = 1356			
accomplished."				476+460+420 = 1356			

Figure 6. Correlation of phrase in Matthew 5:18 with DNA Nucleon Matrix

The next phrase, *"will by any means disappear from the Law"* has a gematria of 2312. There are 15 combinations of numbers from the Nucleon Matrix that add to 2312 (see Appendix 10). Four of those combinations are shown in Figure 7.

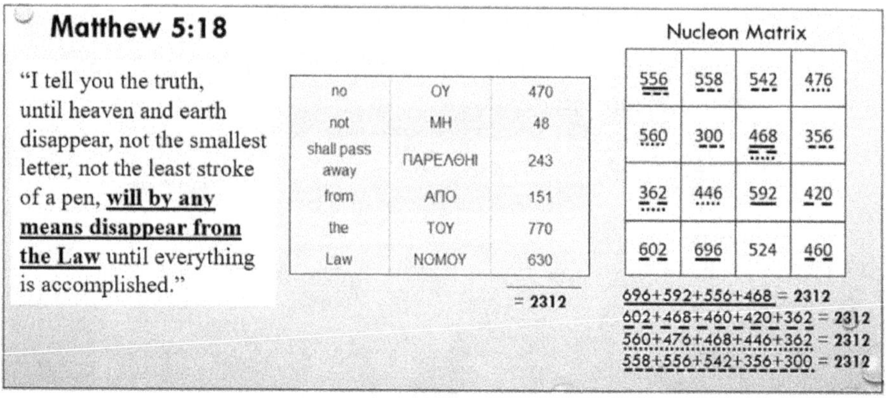

Figure 7. Correlation of phrase in Matthew 5:18 with DNA Nucleon Matrix

And lastly, completing the verse combining the phrases at the beginning and end of the verse, "I tell you the truth," and "until everything is accomplished", the gematria of these phrases is 3406, and there are 39 different combination of numbers from the DNA Nucleon Matrix that add up to 3406 (see Appendix 10). Three of those combinations are shown in Figure 8.

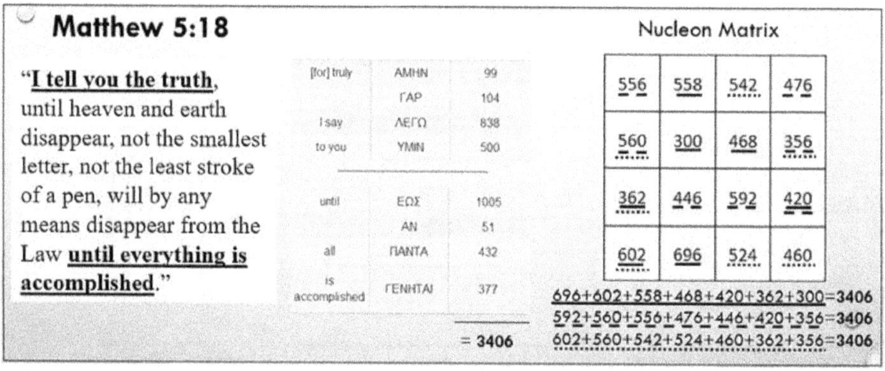

Figure 8. Correlation of remaining phrases in Matthew 5:18 with
DNA Nucleon Matrix.

The Bible is meticulously designed and inspired by God. If you remove even one small letter, the math falls apart. In fact, when I first started looking into this, I used *The Interlinear Bible* by Hendrickson Publishers to get the Hebrew and Greek words. I discovered a discrepancy in John 1:1 in *The Interlinear Bible* that was not in the more accurate original Greek text shown at <u>https://livinggreeknt.org/</u>. The Greek translation in *The Interlinear Bible* was missing one letter in John 1:1, an iota subscript. With that one letter—an iota subscript—missing the entire gematria of John 1:1 collapsed. It no longer equaled 3627 which is 39 x 93. There was no correlation to Genesis 1:1 with that one letter, an iota, missing. Every word, every letter is important. God designed His Word to communicate to us and it is God's truth. It is not a haphazard collection of literature that is meaningless. It is definitely our main connection to our Creator.

Hebrews 1:3

Another key New Testament verse that expresses God sustains all things by His powerful Word is Hebrews 1:3, which in part is: "*The Son is the radiance of God's glory and the exact representation of His being, sustaining all things by His powerful Word. ...*" If you break up this sentence into three parts, a, b and c, there is correlation of all three phrases with the Nucleon Matrix as shown in Figure 9. All numbers of the Nucleon Matrix are used at least once to correlate to Hebrews 1:3.

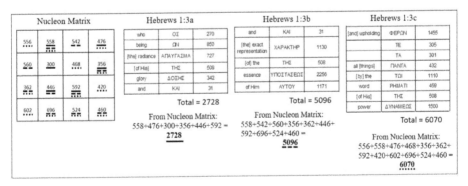

Figure 9. Correlation of Hebrews 1:3 with the DNA Nucleon Matrix.

2 Corinthians 7:10 & 2 Timothy 4:2

There are two verses in the New Testament that have a gematria of 7918, the sum of all the numbers in the Nucleon Matrix. These verses are:

Godly sorrow brings repentance that leads to salvation and leaves no regret, but worldly sorrow brings death.

– 2 Corinthians 7:10

Preach the Word; be prepared in season and out of season; correct, rebuke and encourage—with great patience and careful instruction.

– 2 Timothy 4:2

These verses have a 1:1 correlation with the Nucleon matrix because the gematria of each verse is 7918 and the values of all 16 numbers in the Nucleon Matrix, added together, is 7918. The gematria of these verses is shown in Figure 10.

2 Corinthians 7:10			2 Timothy 4:2		
[for] the	H	8	preach	ΚΗΡΥΞΟΝ	708
	ΓΑΡ	104	the	ΤΟΝ	420
according to	ΚΑΤΑ	322	Word	ΛΟΓΟΝ	223
God	ΘΕΟΝ	134	be ready	ΕΠΙΣΤΗΘΙ	622
grief	ΛΥΠΗ	518	in season	ΕΥΚΑΙΡΩΣ	1536
[produces] repentance	ΜΕΤΑΝΟΙΑΝ	527	[and] out of season	ΑΚΑΙΡΩΣ	1132
unto	ΕΙΣ	215	reprove	ΕΛΕΓΞΟΝ	223
salvation	ΣΩΤΗΡΙΑΝ	1469	rebuke	ΕΠΙΤΙΜΗΣΟΝ	773
without regret	ΑΜΕΤΑΜΕΛΗΤΟΝ	850	[and] exhort	ΠΑΡΑΚΑΛΕΣΟΝ	558
	ΕΡΓΑΖΕΤΑΙ	432	in	ΕΝ	55
	H	8	all	ΠΑΣΗΙ	299
however	ΔΕ	9	patience	ΜΑΚΡΟΘΥΜΙΑΙ	701
the	ΤΟΥ	770	and	ΚΑΙ	31
[of the] world	ΚΟΣΜΟΥ	800	instruction	ΔΙΔΑΧΗΙ	637
grief	ΛΥΠΗ	518			
[produces] death	ΘΑΝΑΤΟΝ	481			7918
	ΚΑΤΕΡΓΑΖΕΤΑΙ	753			
		7918			

Figure 10. Gematria of 2 Corinthians 7:10 and 2 Timothy 4:2

Let this information sink into your mind. The numbers associated with the DNA of all living things correlate to the gematria, the numbers associated with the letters and words of the following verses in the Old and New Testaments:

Genesis 1:1 *In the beginning God created the heavens and the earth.*

Genesis 1:14 *And God said, "Let there be lights in the expanse of the sky to separate the day from the night, and let them serve as signs to mark seasons and days and years."*

Genesis 1:27 *So God created man in His own image, in the image of God He created him; male and female He created them.*

Genesis 2:23 *The man said, "This is now bone of my bones and flesh of my flesh; she shall be called 'woman,' for she was taken out of man."*

John 1:1 *In the beginning was the Word and the Word was with God and the Word was God.*

Colossians 1:17 *He is before all things, and in Him all things hold together.*

Hebrews 1:3a-c *The Son is the radiance of God's glory and the exact representation of His being, sustaining all things by His powerful word.*

2 Corinthians 7:10 *Godly sorrow brings repentance that leads to salvation and leaves no regret, but worldly sorrow brings death.*

2 Timothy 4:2 *Preach the Word; be prepared in season and out of season; correct, rebuke and encourage—with great patience and careful instruction.*

Proverbs 30:6 *Do not add to His words, or He will rebuke you and prove you a liar.*

Matthew 5:18 *I tell you the truth, until heaven and earth disappear, not the smallest letter, not the least stroke of a pen, will by any means disappear from the Law until everything is accomplished.*

Psalms 66:5 *Come and see what God has done, how awesome His works in man's behalf!*

These verses speak of the creation, God's Word, how He holds everything together, and how every word and even every letter in God's Word is important. The human writers of these verses wrote these words as they were inspired by the Holy Spirit. God, our Creator, is the author and designer of these words. I believe the LORD encoded these correlations between the DNA of all living things and His Word for us to discover in the end times, to help many people realize that the Bible is indeed from our Creator and His revelation of Himself to us.

As written in Psalm 66:5 "*Come and see what God has done, how awesome His works in man's behalf!*" Indeed, it is fun discovering hidden secrets in God's Word that reveal His signature and His design. His creation and His Word are awesome!

CHAPTER 8

The Gospel Message

So far, we have looked at twelve verses in the Bible and how the gematria of these verses have various unique mathematical qualities, and how these verses connect mathematically to the molecular structure of DNA. In this chapter we will look at one verse, John 3:16, and show how this verse also is uniquely connected mathematically with Genesis 1:1 and with the DNA Nucleon Matrix of numbers. John 3:16 is a key verse in the New Testament because it sums up the gospel message, the good news of God's Kingdom. John 3:16 states, *"For God so loved the world that He gave His One and Only Son that whoever believes in Him shall not perish but have everlasting life."*

John 3:16 is a key verse of God's message to us. Sin has separated us from God. The scripture says, *"The wages of sin is death."* (Romans 6:23) God is a loving God who cares about each one of us. But He is also a holy God and a God of justice. The only way He can be both loving and just is to pay the penalty for sin on our behalf. So, Jesus, the Son of God, born of a virgin, came from heaven into the earth realm as a human being, lived a perfect life, and then died for our sins. In the greatest legal transaction ever, Jesus paved the way for God to remain just and to justly forgive the sins of those who choose to receive the gift that Jesus died to give us. We put our trust in Him and we no longer have to be separated from God for eternity, we get to have eternal life with Him.

The gematria of John 3:16 is 13,690. If you add up each letter to get the gematria for each word and then add up all the words, the number you get is 13,690. Is this number significant? Well, it is 37 x 370. The number 37 is a key number in Genesis 1:1, with a gematria of 2701, which equals 37 x 73. Separating John 3:16 into three parts, Figure 1 shows the correlation of John 3:16 with the DNA Nucleon Matrix. Every one of the 16 numbers in the Nucleon Matrix is used at least once, and the only number used all three times is 592, which is the only number that is a multiple of 37 (37 x 16).

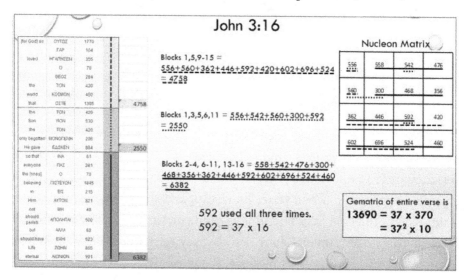

Figure 1. Correlation of John 3:16 with the Nucleon Matrix.

The Nucleon Matrix has a greater connection to John 3:16 than just these three combinations, though. As it turns out there are nine combinations of numbers from the Nucleon Matrix that add up to 4758—the phrase marked with a dashed line in Figure 2, seven combinations of numbers that add up to 2550—the phrase marked with a dotted line in Figure 2, and three combinations of numbers that add up to 6382—the phrase marked with a solid line in Figure 2.

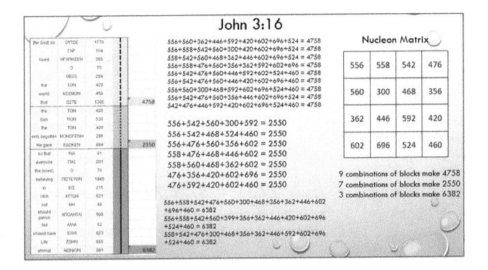

Figure 2. Additional correlation between John 3:16 and the DNA Nucleon Matrix

The connection between John 3:16 and the Nucleon Matrix is even more firmly established with these multiple combinations of numbers that add up to the phrases of John 3:16.

There is something even more amazing about John 3:16 and how it connects mathematically with Genesis 1:1. Figure 3 below shows the gematria of John 3:16, along with the gematria of Genesis 1:1. It is possible to add five words from John 3:16 to equal the gematria of Genesis 1:1, 2701.

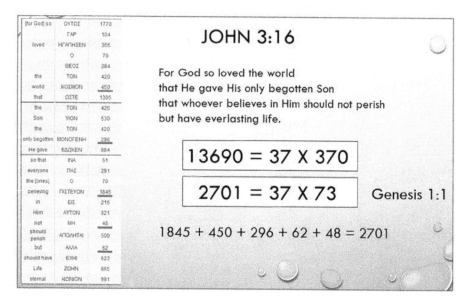

[for God] so	OYTΩΣ	1770
	ΓAP	104
loved	HΓAΠHΣEN	355
	O	70
	ΘEOΣ	284
the	TON	420
world	KOΣMON	450
that	ΩΣTE	1305
the	TON	420
Son	YION	530
the	TON	420
only begotten	MONOΓENH	296
He gave	EΔΩKEN	884
so that	INA	61
everyone	ΠAΣ	281
the [ones]	O	70
believing	ΠIΣTEYΩN	1845
in	EIΣ	215
Him	AYTON	821
not	MH	48
should perish	AΠOΛHTAI	500
but	AΛΛA	62
should have	EXHI	623
Life	ZΩHN	865
eternal	AIΩNION	991

JOHN 3:16

For God so loved the world
that He gave His only begotten Son
that whoever believes in Him should not perish
but have everlasting life.

$$13690 = 37 \times 370$$

$$2701 = 37 \times 73$$ Genesis 1:1

$$1845 + 450 + 296 + 62 + 48 = 2701$$

Figure 3. Correlation of John 3:16 gematria with Genesis 1:1 gematria.

The fact that there are these five words from John 3:16 that add up to gematria of Genesis 1:1 is no big deal. But incredibly there are 248 different combinations of numbers in John 3:16, using a word only once in each combination, that add up to 2701. Appendix 11 shows these combinations. In order to confirm that not any combination of numbers is repeated, I start with the largest number in the gematria of John 3:16, which is the word translated "believing" that adds up to 1845 and show all the combinations of numbers using 1845 that add up to 2701. Then I take all the combinations of words starting with the second largest word, the first word of the verse, with a gematria of 1770. In some combinations, you will see the number 70 twice. But the Greek word "O" with a gematria of 70 is listed twice in John 3:16. Likewise, the Greek word "TON", which is translated "the" has a gematria of 420 and is listed three times in John 3:16.

If you look carefully at these 248 different combinations of numbers from John 3:16 that add up to 2701, there are some symbolic patterns of numbers that emerge.

- There are five sequences of numbers that begin with 1845. The number five is symbolic of God's grace, God's favor and forgiveness for the unworthy. The Lord's grace and forgiveness is present in the Tabernacle, where provision was made for the forgiveness of sin. Nearly every measurement of the Tabernacle is a multiple of five. The sacred anointing oil is made up of five parts; 1) 500 shekels myrrh, 2) 250 shekels cinnamon, 3) 250 shekels calamus, 4) 500 shekels cassia, and 5) a hin of olive oil. The apostle John wrote five books centered on the grace of God and eternal life (the gospel of John, 1 John, 2 John, 3 John and Revelation). Jesus multiplied five loaves of bread to feed 5000. John 3:16 speaks of God's grace.

- There are seven sequences of numbers that begin with 1770. The number 7 signifies spiritual perfection and completeness.

- There are 26 sequences of numbers that begin with 1305. The number 26 is the gematria of LORD in Hebrew.

- There are 45 sequences of numbers that begin with 884. The number 45 is a multiple of 5.

- There are 42 sequences of numbers that begin with 865. The number 42 is a multiple of 7.

- There are 24 sequences of numbers that begin with 623. 24 represents the 12 Tribes of Israel and the 12 Disciples of Jesus.

- There are 14 sequences of numbers that begin with 530. The number 14 is a multiple of 7.

- There are five sequences of numbers that begin with 500, again highlighting God's grace.

It is significant and amazing to see the mathematical connection between Genesis 1:1 and John 3:16. We have a Creator, He loves us, and we can have eternal life if we believe and receive the gift of His dying for our sins. He planned for Jesus' provision for our salvation from the beginning. If you have never understood this message and are understanding it now for the first time, I invite you to speak out loud in prayer and thank Jesus for dying for your sins and invite Jesus into your life, that your sins may be forgiven and you will be born again, spiritually, and live forever with God in heaven.

CHAPTER 9

I AM Statements in the Bible

Looking at more of the Old Testament and New Testament verses, this chapter will cover the numerical significance of the "I AM" statements in the Bible. The information in this chapter comes from John Nuyten's website, www.thelivingword.org.au from Session 12 "I AM" the door. I have verified his work and it is presented here.

Old Testament

The most well-known "I AM" statement in the Bible is from Exodus when Moses asked God who he should say sent him when he told the Israelites that God had sent him to deliver them. God answered Moses:

> "*I AM WHO I AM. This is what you are to say to the Israelites:*
> '*I AM has sent me to you.*'"
>
> – *Exodus 3:14*

In Hebrew the phrase I AM is pronounced "ahaya" and is made up of 4 Hebrew letters:

$$\text{ה י ה א}$$

These 4 Hebrew letters exist in the Old Testament as a word exactly 37 times. The verb tense changes so that the English translation varies from:

I am

I will be

I was

I have been.

But in Hebrew it's the exact same four letters. Some of these occurrences start with the letter "Vav" which means "and", but then are followed by the four letters representing God's presence. The Table below shows the verses where these four letters occur as a word in the Old Testament. It occurs in 13 of the Old Testament books, written by at least 11 different human authors over a span of about a thousand years. It is significant that there are 37 occurrences of this Hebrew word which represents the Lord and which is shown to be a significant number in the first verse of the Bible. The 37 occurrences of these 4 Hebrew letters are shown in Table 1.

Table 1. Occurrences of "I AM" in the Old Testament

אהיה

	Verse	Significance and excerpt
1	Genesis 26:3	First occurrence. The LORD says to Isaac "and I will be with you and bless you..."
2	Genesis 31:3	The LORD says to Jacob "and I will be with you."
3	Exodus 3:12	God says to Moses "for I will be with you...."
4, 5, 6	Exodus 3:14	God uses the I AM phrase 3 times in the one verse: "I AM WHO I AM.... I AM has sent me to you."
7	Exodus 4:12	God says to Moses "And now go, and I will be with your mouth and will teach you..."
8	Exodus 4:15	God speaking to Moses and Aaron: "And I will be with your mouth, and with his mouth..."
9	Deut 31:23	The LORD says to Joshua "I myself will be with you."
10	Joshua 1:5	The LORD says to Joshua "...as I was with Moses, I will be with you..."
11	Joshua 3:7	The LORD says to Joshua "...as I was with Moses, I am with you."
12	Judges 6:16	The LORD tells Gideon "I will be with you"
13	2 Samuel 7:6	The LORD says to David "but I have been moving about in a tent..."
14	2 Samuel 7:9	The LORD says to David "And I have been with you wherever you went and cut off all your
15	2 Samuel 7:14	The LORD says to David, of his seed: "I shall be a father to him, and he shall be a son to me."
16	1 Chron 17:5	The LORD says to Nathan the prophet who tells David: "but I have been from tent to tent ..."
17	1 Chron 17:8	The LORD says to David through Nathan: "and I have been with you wherever you have walked..."
18	1 Chron 17:13	The LORD says to David through Nathan: "I will be his father, and he will be my son."
19	1 Chron 28:6	David speaking what the LORD had said "And He said to me, your son Solomon shall build My house and My courts, for I have chosen him as a son to Me, and I surely will be a Father to him.
20	Psalm 50:21	God speaking of the wicked: "you thought I would be like yourself..."
21	Isaiah 3:7	The LORD is saying "not will I be one who binds up..."
22	Jeremiah 11:4	The LORD speaking to Judah through Jeremiah: "...you shall be my people, and I will be your God."
23	Jeremiah 24:7	"And I will give them a heart to know me, that I am the LORD. And they shall be my people, and I will be their God. ..."
24	Jeremiah 30:22	"And you shall be my people; and I will be your God."
25	Jeremiah 31:1	The LORD says "I will be the God of all the families of Israel, and they shall be my people."
26	Jeremiah 32:38	"And they shall be my people, and I will be their God."
27	Ezekiel 11:20	"And they shall be to me for a people, and I will be to them for God."
28	Ezekiel 14:11	"...but they are to me for a people, and I will be to them for God, ..."
29	Ezekiel 34:24	"And I the LORD will be to them God..."
30	Ezekiel 36:28	"... And you shall be to me a people, and I will be to you God."
31	Ezekiel 37:23	"...and I will cleanse them. So shall they be to me for a people, and I will be to them for God.
32	Hosea 1:9	"Then He said, Call his name Not-My-People; for you are not My people and I will not be for you."
33	Hosea 11:4	"...And I was to them as those who lift off the yoke on their jaws..."
34	Hosea 14:5	"I will be as the dew to Israel; he shall blossom as the lily, and cast out his roots in Lebanon."
35,36	Zechariah 2:5	"For I will be to her a wall of fire all around, and I will be for glory in her midst..."
37	Zechariah 8:8	"... And they shall be for a people to me, and I will be their God,..."

Is it a coincidence that these 4 letters that represent what God called Himself, I AM, exist 37 times in the Old Testament? Or does it point to inspiration of the Scriptures and intentional design for Moses, Joshua, Samuel, Ezra, David, Solomon, Isaiah, Jeremiah, Ezekiel, Hosea and Zechariah to use this word for a total of 37 times? I view these 37 occurrences as intentional, not coincidental, and further evidence that the entire Old Testament is inspired by God.

It is also interesting to note that the gematria of this word "I AM" is 21, which is 3 x 7. The triune God (3) times spiritual perfection and completeness (7). Also, remember that 21 x 37 = 777, another number representing the triune God. It all fits together with such order.

New Testament

In the New Testament, 'I am" statements by or about Jesus also exist 37 times. The Greek words for I AM are:

$$\text{ΕΓΩ ΕΙΜΙ}$$

This word combination is found in the New Testament 37 times. The Bible version that I commonly use is the NIV version. In the NIV version there are more than 37 occurrences of the phrase "I am" in English in the New Testament, but in Greek, these seven letters making up these two words are in the New Testament exactly 37 times. Table 2 below shows the 37 occurrences of the seven letters/two words that translate "I am".

	Verse	Excerpt
1	Matt 14:27	Jesus said to them, "Be comforted, I AM! Do not fear"
2	Matt 22:32	"I AM the God of Abraham, Isaac and Jacob."
3	Mark 6:50	"Have courage, I AM! Do not fear"
4	Mark 14:62	...and Jesus said "I AM! And you will see the Son of man sitting at the right hand of power..."
5	Luke 22:70	Are you the Son of God? He replied, "You are right in saying I AM."
6	Luke 24:39	"Look at my hands and my feet that I AM!"
7	John 4:26	Jesus said to her, "I AM, the One speaking to you."
8	John 6:20	Jesus said to them "I AM! Do not fear."
9	John 6:35	Then Jesus declared, "I AM the Bread of Life...."
10	John 6:41	the Jews began to grumble because he said, "I AM the bread that came down from heaven."
11	John 6:48	"I AM the Bread of Life."
12	John 6:51	"I AM the living bread that came down from heaven..."
13	John 8:12	"I AM the Light of the World."
14	John 8:18	"I AM the one who testifies for myself"
15	John 8:24	"If you do not believe that I AM, you will die in your sins."
16	John 8:28	"When you have lifted up the Son of Man, then you will know that I AM"
17	John 8:58	"I tell you the truth," Jesus answered, "before Abraham was born, I AM!"
18	John 10:7	"I tell you the truth, I AM the door for the sheep."
19	John 10:9	"I AM the Door; whoever enters through me will be saved."
20	John 10:11	"I AM the Good Shepherd. The good shepherd lays down his life for the sheep."
21	John 10:14	"I AM the Good Shepherd"
22	John 11:25	Jesus said to her, "I AM the Resurrection and the Life."
23	John 13:19	"I am telling you now before it happens, so that when it happens you may believe that I AM."
24	John 14:6	Jesus answered, "I AM the Way and the Truth and the Life."
25	John 15:1	"I AM the True Vine, and my Father is the gardener."
26	John 15:5	"I AM the Vine; you are the branches."
27	John 18:5	Jesus said, "I AM he!"
28	John 18:6	When Jesus said "I AM he", they drew back and fell to the ground.
29	John 18:8	"I told you that I AM he" Jesus answered
30	Acts 9:5	"I AM Jesus whom you persecute"
31	Acts 18:10	"Do not be silent because I AM with you"
32	Acts 22:8	"I AM Jesus the Nazarene, whom you persecute"
33	Acts 26:15	"I AM Jesus, whom you persecute"
34	Rev 1:8	"I AM the Alpha and the Omega" says the Lord God
35	Rev 1:17	"...Do not be afraid. I AM the First and the Last and the Living One..."
36	Rev 2:23	"Then all the churches will know that I AM the One who searches hearts and minds..."
37	Rev 22:16	"I AM the Root and the Offspring of David, and the bright Morning Star."

Table 2. Occurrences of "I AM" in the New Testament

Jesus' use of the phrase "I am ..." is significant because that is exactly why the majority of the Jewish leaders wanted Jesus dead because they thought he was committing blasphemy by claiming to be God. When the Jews said to Jesus, "*You are not yet fifty years old, and you have seen Abraham!*" (John 8:57), Jesus replied to them: "*I tell you the truth, before Abraham was born, I am!*" (John 8:58) Unfortunately, what the Jewish leaders at that time missed is that He *was* God in the flesh, but came initially as Savior for the purpose of the salvation of mankind from their sins. At His second coming

He will fulfill all the prophecies of His coming as King. The fact that this phrase exists 37 times in the New Testament is another indicator that both the Old and New Testaments are inspired by God.

There is one more fact I'd like to share that gives evidence that the entire Old and New Testaments are inspired by God. The first chapter of Genesis, the first book of the Old Testament, Genesis 1, has 434 Hebrew words.[1] The last chapter of Revelation, the last book of the New Testament, Revelation 22 has 454 Greek words.[2] If you add up these words 434 + 454, it sums to 888, the gematria for Jesus. Jesus is the Word (John 1:1, 12) and Jesus is the First and the Last (Revelation 1:17, Revelation 22:13). The number of words add up precisely to 888 out of intentional design. As the Lord says in Proverbs 30:6 "*Do not add to His words or He will rebuke you and prove you a liar.*"

I have demonstrated mathematical phenomena in several verses of the Old and New Testament that give solid evidence that the Bible has designed numerical qualities and connection to the DNA of all living things. I have also presented information to show the entire Bible, Old Testament and New Testament, has intentional design. It would be illogical to believe that these factual mathematical connections are by "chance". It is much more logical to accept that we have a Creator, and the Bible is God's written revelation of Himself to us, created in His image.

SECTION 2

THE EVIDENCE OF PROPHECY

The Bible gives evidence of inspiration from God by the prophetic nature of verses scattered throughout the Old and New Testament. As stated in Isaiah, God says:

> "I am God, and there is no other; I am God, and there is none like me. **I make known the end from the beginning,** from ancient times, what is still to come. I say: My purpose will stand, and I will do all that I please."
>
> – Isaiah 46:9-10

I watched an episode of the Daystar network's *Joni Table Talk* with guest Troy Brewer. He was explaining how time in God's perspective is like looking at a train from the sky. From the vantage point of the sky, you can see the beginning of the train and the end of the train at the same time. From the vantage point of the ground, you can see only one portion of the train at any given time. Prophecy is possible because God sees the end from the beginning. Mankind cannot predict the future accurately hundreds and thousands of years away, but God can, and He has made known certain things to the prophets as recorded in the Bible. Prophecy fulfilled is proof the prophet's words did come from God.

Much of the Old Testament was written by prophets of God and contains detailed prophecy about future events. Some of the prophecies have been fulfilled while others are yet to come. There are 16 books in the Old Testament from prophets in Israel. The four "major prophets" are Isaiah, Jeremiah, Ezekiel and Daniel, and there are 12 smaller books from prophets, referred to as the "minor prophets".

Additionally, throughout other parts of the Old Testament, there are prophecies strategically placed beginning in Genesis, in the Psalms, and scattered throughout the Old Testament. The New Testament contains prophecies as well, especially the last book of the New Testament, Revelation. It would take volumes to look at each prophecy, which ones have been fulfilled and which ones are still to be fulfilled. For the purposes of this book, to prove that prophecy is an evidence that the Bible is inspired by God, I have picked three major themes of prophecy to examine:

1. History of nations and political power from the Babylonian empire to the time of Christ.

2. Jesus Christ's coming to earth as the promised Messiah, as Savior for our sins.

3. The return of Jewish people to a restored Israel from all over the earth.

By choosing these three topics, we can look at the detailed prophetic history that was fulfilled before Christ, prophecies that foretold the coming of Christ, and modern-day fulfillment of prophecy with the recent re-establishment of Israel as a nation. These fulfilled prophecies are only possible because God, who knows the "end from the beginning" revealed these things in advance through His Word in the Bible.

CHAPTER 10

Prophecy of Kingdoms from the Babylonian Empire to the Time of Christ

The Bible prophesies the kingdoms to come and battles of political power after the Babylonian empire in the Book of Daniel. Daniel gives astounding detailed prophecies about coming kingdoms, including outcomes of battles, dynasty succession drama, political alliances and marriages from the time of the Babylonian Captivity until nearly the coming of Christ, a period of about 600 years.

Daniel was taken to Babylon from Jerusalem in 605 BC when King Nebuchadnezzar of the Babylonians besieged Jerusalem. The Israelites who were taken to Babylon either died in Babylon or lived 70 years during the period of captivity before they were allowed to return to Israel under the rule of Cyrus, King of Persia.

Daniel supernaturally interpreted Nebuchadnezzar's dream as recorded in the second chapter of Daniel. King Nebuchadnezzar asked his wise men to tell him what his dream was and interpret its meaning. Did you catch that? King Nebuchadnezzar didn't tell his wisemen the dream and ask for their interpretation. He asked them to tell him what he dreamed and then give the interpretation. He decided he would believe their interpretation if they could tell him *what* he had dreamed. None of the wise men of Babylon could do that and were to be executed.

But Daniel prayed to the LORD and the LORD revealed Neb's dream to Daniel. He was able to tell Nebuchadnezzar what his dream was and its true interpretation. The interpretation of the dream revealed the current kingdom along with major empires to come in the future. Daniel told King Nebuchadnezzar what his dream was as recorded in the second chapter of Daniel:

> *You looked, O king, and there before you stood a large statue— an enormous, dazzling statue, awesome in appearance. The head of the statue was made of pure gold, its chest and arms of silver, its belly and thighs of bronze, its legs of iron, its feet partly of iron and partly of baked clay. While you were watching, a rock was cut out, but not by human hands. It struck the statue on its feet of iron and clay and smashed them. Then the iron, the clay, the bronze, the silver and the gold were broken to pieces at the same time and became like chaff on a threshing floor in the summer. The wind swept them away without leaving a trace. But the rock that struck the statue became a huge mountain and filled the whole earth.*
>
> *– Daniel 2:31-35*

When Daniel was shown Nebuchadnezzar's dream, Daniel did not have a lucky guess. The LORD specifically gave the dream to Nebuchadnezzar and Daniel because it was a prophetic dream. God, Himself, wanted it to be known that its message was from the One and Only True God. God showed Daniel the dream, and with that miracle, Nebuchadnezzar believed the interpretation. Daniel recorded the event, the king's dream and the interpretation for future generations, including us right now.

After Daniel reveals King Nebuchadnezzar's dream, he is given a place of prominence in the current kingdom. He gives the dream's interpretation in Daniel 2. This prophecy is a general overview of world history from the time of Babylonian Empire through to the Roman Empire, as well as a brief look at the end times and the final Kingdom to come which will endure forever.

This was the dream, and now we will interpret it to the king.

You, O king, are the king of kings. The God of heaven has given you dominion and power and might and glory; in your hands he has placed mankind and the beasts of the field and the birds of the air. Wherever they live, he has made you ruler over them all. You are that head of gold.

After you, another kingdom will rise, inferior to yours. Next, a third kingdom, one of bronze, will rule over the whole earth.

Finally, there will be a fourth kingdom, strong as iron—for iron breaks and smashes everything—and as iron breaks things to pieces, so it will crush and break all the others. Just as you saw that the feet and toes were partly of baked clay and partly of iron, so this will be a divided kingdom; yet it will have some of the strength of iron in it, even as you saw iron mixed with clay. As the toes were partly iron and partly clay, so this kingdom will be partly strong and partly brittle. And just as you saw the iron mixed with baked clay, so the people will be a mixture and will not remain united, any more than iron mixes with clay.

In the time of those kings, the God of heaven will set up a kingdom that will never be destroyed nor will it be left to another people. It will crush all those kingdoms and bring them to an end, but it will itself endure forever.

*This is the meaning of the vision of the rock cut out of a mountain, but not by human hands—a rock that broke the iron, the bronze, the clay, the silver and the gold to pieces. **The great God has shown the king what will take place in the future. The dream is true and the interpretation is trustworthy.***

— Daniel 2:36-45

We know from history that the first kingdom, represented by the head of gold is the Babylonian empire, the second kingdom is the Medo-Persian empire, the third kingdom is Greece, and the fourth kingdom is the Roman empire. The end of the dream is a prophetic event that has not yet been fulfilled when God, Himself will set up His Kingdom that will never be destroyed.

Daniel 7 records another dream of Daniel's that also gives a general overview of future kingdoms to come. In his dream Daniel saw four beasts: The Lion, Bear, Leopard and a terrifying and frightening Beast. Daniel 7:17 states *"The four great beasts are four kingdoms that will rise from the earth."* He expands on the fourth beast with prophecy of the end times that has not yet been fulfilled. The four beasts correlate to the four major kingdoms of Babylon, Medo-Persia, Greece and Rome.

In Daniel 8, Daniel records another vision that gives more detail about the second and third kingdoms likened to a ram and a goat. Figure 1 shows the major empires from Daniel 2, Daniel 7 and Daniel 8.

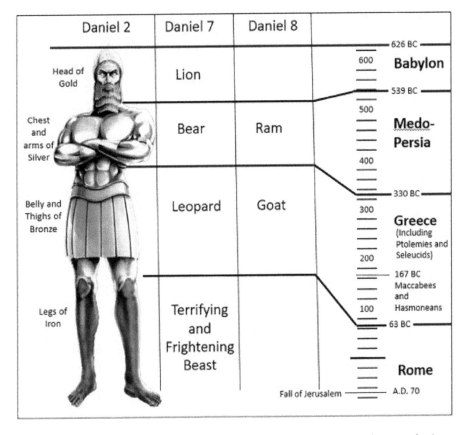

Figure 1. Four major kingdoms of the earth as prophesied in Daniel 2, 7 and 8.[1]

Daniel gives the interpretation of the vision of the ram and the goat as symbolizing the Medo-Persian Empire and Greece:

> *The **two-horned ram that you saw represents the kings of Media and Persia. The shaggy goat is the king of Greece,** and the large horn between his eyes is the first king. The four horns that replaced the one that was broken off represent four kingdoms that will emerge from his nation but will not have the same power.*
>
> *— Daniel 8:20-22*

Daniel prophesies that after the Babylonian kingdom, the kings of Media and Persia will take over the Babylonian's and then Greece will take over the Medes and the Persians. The first king of Greece will be replaced by four kingdoms with not as much power. We know from history that the large horn of the shaggy goat, the first king, is Alexander the Great. He became the King of Greece at age 20 in 336 BC and expanded the kingdom from Greece to northwestern India until his sudden death at the age of 33. His empire was divided among his four generals (the four horns that replaced the one that was broken off):

- Lysimachus, who took Thrace and much of Asia Minor

- Cassander, who controlled Macedonia and Greece

- Ptolemy I – ruled Egypt, Palestine (formerly Israel), Cilicia, Petra and Cyprus. He founded the Ptolemaic Dynasty which lasted until the death of Cleopatra VII in 30 BC.

- Seleucos I – ruled the remainder of Asia and founded the Seleucid Empire which was comprised of Mesopotamia, the Levant, Persia and part of India.

Daniel 11 gives a lot more prophetic detail about the coming kingdoms of the Medes/Persians, Greece and Rome. It is amazing the detail he gives and the accuracy of what occurred in history from the time of Cyrus the Great, King of Persia until nearly the time of Christ. Daniel 10:1 sets the stage and reveals that Daniel was given the revelation of the future in *the third year of Cyrus, King of Persia*, which would have been 557 B.C. That Cyrus was Cyrus II, also known as Cyrus the Great, who reigned over Persia from 559-530 BC and was the first emperor of the Achaemenid Empire (Persian Empire).[2] The prophetic revelation that was given to Daniel is recorded in Daniel 11, beginning in verse 2 with the kings and kingdoms that would follow Cyrus II through 164 B.C.

Now then, I tell you the truth: Three more kings will appear in Persia, and then a fourth, who will be far richer than all the others.

*When he has gained power by his wealth, he will stir up
everyone against the kingdom of Greece.*

– Daniel 11:2

The first of the three kings that reigned in Persia after Cyrus the Great was his son, Cambyses II who ruled from 530-522 B.C.[3] Darius I, cousin of Cambyses, took the throne from 522-486 BC.[4] However, less well known, there was another king that ruled between Cambyses and Darius in 522. According to Livius.org, articles on ancient history, when King Cambyses was conquering Egypt, someone calling himself Smerdis became sole ruler of the Achaemenid empire after Cambyses died of natural causes. According to a Behistun inscription, this Smerdis' rule started on 11 March 522 BCE, corroborated by the dating of letters in Babylonia. On July 1 he formally became king. He was killed by Darius on 29 September in a stronghold in Media called Sikayauvati. Darius claimed that he was not the real Smerdis, but a rebel who was a look-alike named Gaumata. This man was a Magian (Mede).[5] He ruled only for a couple of months.

The fourth king was Xerxes I (486-465 BC), also referred to as Xerxes the Great, who attempted to conquer Greece in 480 BC.[6]

So, Daniel prophesied correctly that after Cyrus, who was the King of Persia when Daniel was living, there would be three more kings and then a fourth king who would be richer and greater than the others and who would come against the kingdom of Greece.

Daniel continues his prophetic words:

*Then **a mighty king will appear**, who will rule with great
power and do as he pleases. After he has appeared, **his empire
will be broken up and parceled out toward the four winds
of heaven**. It will not go to his descendants, nor will it have
the power he exercised, because his empire will be uprooted and
given to others.*

– Daniel 11:3-4

The **mighty king who appeared** was Alexander the Great, who ruled from 336-323 BC, over the kingdom of Greece. And as noted previously, in Daniel 8, his kingdom was divided among his four generals. There is a gap in time of unrecorded events before the first word, "Then" in Daniel 11:3. Between Xerxes the Great's reign which ended in 465 BC and Alexander the Great's reign which began in 336 BC, there were seven more kings who reigned in the Achaemenid Empire. The kings not referred to in Daniel's prophetic statement of Daniel 11 are: Artaxerxes I who reigned 465-424 BC,[7] Xerxes II, who had a 45-day reign in 424 BC,[8] Darius II who reigned 423-404 BC,[9] Artaxerxes II Mnemon who reigned 404-358 BC,[10] Artaxerxes III who reigned 358-338 BC,[11] Arses (Artaxerxes IV) who reigned from November 338 – June 336 BC,[12] and Darius III, the last king of the Achaemenid Empire who reigned from 336-330 BC.[13]

Alexander the Great was far mightier than the previous kings mentioned. He became king of Greece at the age of 20 and by the age of 30, he had created one of the largest empires of the ancient world, stretching from Greece to northwestern India. He was undefeated in battle and is widely considered one of history's most successful military commanders. He invaded the Achaemenid Empire beginning in 334 BC and captured the capital of the Achaemenid Empire, Persepolis in 330 BC.[14] At Alexander the Great's death in 323 BC the kingdom of Greece was broken up to Alexander's four generals, Lysimachus, Cassander, Ptolemy I and Seleucos I. Following these prophecies Daniel goes on to prophesy the exact history of political power in much detail until nearly the time of Christ. From Daniel 11:5 through Daniel 11:29, Daniel prophesies much detail concerning the Ptolemaic vs. Seleucid dynasties. He refers to the Ptolemaic Dynasty as "the king of the South" and the Seleucid Dynasty as the "king of the North".

> *The king of the South will become strong, but one of his commanders will become even stronger than he and will rule his own kingdom with great power.*
>
> *– Daniel 11:5*

Although Alexander the Great's kingdom, the Hellenistic Empire, was divided among his four generals, two of the generals emerged with the most power and territory. *The King of the South* was Ptolemy I Soter. He was one of the generals of Alexander the Great, became ruler of Egypt (323-285 BC), and founded the Ptolemaic dynasty.[15] The other King was Seleucus I Nicator (312-281 BC) who was one of the generals of Alexander the Great and established the Seleucid Empire. The phrase *his own kingdom* was Anatolia, Mesopotamia, Syria, Persia and eastern part of empire to India.[16] The prophetic timeline continues:

> *After some years, they will become allies. **The daughter of the** **king of the South** will go to **the king of the North** to make an* **alliance**, *but she will not retain her power, and he and his power will not last. In those days she will be handed over, together with her royal escort and her father and the one who supported her.*
>
> *— Daniel 11:6*

The daughter of the king of the South was Berenice, daughter of Ptolemy II Philadelphus (285-246 BC) of Egypt.[17] ***The king of the North*** was Antiochus II Theos (261-246 BC) of Syria. The ***alliance*** was a treaty cemented by the marriage of Antiochus II to Berenice. Antiochus's former wife, Laodice, conspired to have Antiochus, Berenice and Berenice's son put to death. It is presumed that she poisoned Antiochus. She had Berenice and her son murdered in the late summer of 246 BC.[18] Berenice's father, Ptolemy II also died in 246 BC.[19] I could not find in any historical record how Ptolemy II died, but I find it interesting that he died in 246 BC, the same year that Antiochus II, Berenice and Berenice's son died, at the hands of Laodice. Perhaps Laodice also killed Ptolemy II, but historical records were not kept that he died at the hands of a woman. And the drama continues:

> *One from her family line will arise to take her place. He will attack the forces of the king of the North and enter his fortress; he will fight against them and be victorious.*
>
> *— Daniel 11:7*

Berenice's brother, Ptolemy III Euergetes (246-222 BC) of Egypt, was outraged at Berenice's murder. He attacked *the king of the North* which was Seleucus II Callinicus (246-225),[20] Laodice's son, in Antioch. In this Third Syrian War, Ptolemy also captured Laodice and had her killed.[21]

> *He will also seize their gods, their metal images and their valuable articles of silver and gold and carry them off to Egypt. For some years he will leave the king of the North alone.*
>
> *— Daniel 11:8*

Ptolemy III returned to Egypt in 245 BC, reputedly taking with him 40,000 talents of gold and the statues of Egyptian gods which had been looted centuries before by the Persians.[22] And in 241 BC, Ptolemy made peace with the Seleucids retaining all the conquered territory in Asia Minor and northern Syria.[22]

> *Then the king of the North will invade the realm of the king of the South but will retreat to his own country. His sons will prepare for war and assemble a great army, which will sweep on like an irresistible flood and carry the battle as far as his fortress.*
>
> *— Daniel 11:9-10*

Seleucus II (king of the North) *sons* were Seleucus III Ceraunus who reigned from 225-222 BC and Antiochus III the Great 222-187 BC. Seleucus III unsuccessfully continued his father's war in Asia Minor against Attalus of Pergamon. He was assassinated by members of his army in Anatolia.[23] Antiochus III the Great led campaigns in the Fourth Syrian War in 219 – 218 BC and recaptured territory almost to Ptolemaic Kingdom.

> *Then the king of the South will march out in a rage and fight against the king of the North, who will raise a large army, but it will be defeated. When the army is carried off, the king of*

the South will be filled with pride and will slaughter many thousands, yet he will not remain triumphant.

– Daniel 11:11-12

Ptolemy IV (king of the South), who reigned in Egypt from 221-204 BC, defeated Antiochus (king of the North) at the Battle of Raphia in 217 BC in southern Palestine.[24] Antiochus III lost nearly 10,000 infantrymen at the battle at Raphia, against the king of the South, Ptolemy IV.[25]

For the king of the North will muster another army, larger than the first; and after several years, he will advance with a huge army fully equipped. In those times many will rise against the king of the South. The violent men among your own people will rebel in fulfillment of the vision, but without success.

– Daniel 11:13-14

During the Fifth Syrian War (202-195 BC) Antiochus III took advantage of the death of Ptolemy IV in 204 BC, with Ptolemy V, a child, ruler. He conquered the Ptolemies' territories in Asia Minor and invaded Palestine in 201 BC. Jews joined the forces of Antiochus III, but then the Ptolemaic general Scopas crushed the rebellion in the winter of 201/200 BC.[26]

Then the king of the North will come and build up siege ramps and will capture a fortified city. The forces of the South will be powerless to resist; even their best troops will not have the strength to stand. The invader will do as he pleases; no one will be able to stand against him. He will establish himself in the Beautiful Land and will have the power to destroy it.

– Daniel 11:15-16

Antiochus III then defeated the Ptolemies at the Battle of Panium (200 BC) near the head of the River Jordan. He also captured the Mediterranean port city of Sidon.[27] He was in control of all the region of *the Beautiful Land* (formerly Judah and Israel), by 197 BC.[28]

> *He will determine to come with the might of his entire kingdom and will make an alliance with the king of the South. And he will give him a daughter in marriage in order to overthrow the kingdom, but his plans will not succeed or help him.*
>
> *– Daniel 11:17*

Antiochus III gave his daughter Cleopatra I, at 10 years old in marriage to Ptolemy V, age 16 in 193 BC.[29]

> *Then he will turn his attention to the coastlands and will take many of them, but a commander will put an end to his insolence and will turn his insolence back upon him. After this, he will turn back toward the fortresses of his own country but will stumble and fall, to be seen no more.*
>
> *– Daniel 11:18-19*

Antiochus III secured coast towns which belonged to the remnants of Ptolemaic overseas dominions and the independent Greek cities.[30] He established a footing in Thrace in 196 BC and he invaded the mainland of Greece in 192 BC.[30] But then, the Roman commander, Consul Lucius Cornelius Scipio Asiaticus, defeated Antiochus III at Magnesia in Asia Minor in 190 B.C.[30] Antiochus died in 187 BC.[30]

> *His successor will send out a tax collector to maintain the royal splendor. In a few years, however, he will be destroyed, yet not in anger or in battle.*
>
> *– Daniel 11:20*

Seleucus IV Philopator became ruler of the Seleucid Empire upon his father's, Atiochus III, death in 187 BC. In the Treaty of Apamea with Rome, one year before the death of Antiochus, the Seleucids had to pay Rome for losses in war damage, including 12,000 Euboic talents over the next twelve years.[31] In an effort to collect money to pay the Romans, Seleucus sent his minister Heliodorus (tax collector) to Jerusalem to seize the Jewish temple treasury.[32] On his return from Jerusalem, Heliodorus assassinated Seleucus on September 3, 175 BC.[32]

> *He will be succeeded by a contemptible person who has not been given the honor of royalty. He will invade the kingdom when its people feel secure, and he will seize it through intrigue.*
>
> *— Daniel 11:21*

Seleucus's younger brother, Antiochus IV Epiphanes (175-164 B.C.) seized power when the rightful heir to the throne was the young son of Seleucus (later to become Demetrius I).[33]

> *Then an overwhelming army will be swept away before him; both it and a prince of the covenant will be destroyed.*
>
> *— Daniel 11:22*

The "prince of the covenant" who was destroyed was the Jewish High Priest, Onias III.[34]

> *After coming to an agreement with him, he will act deceitfully and with only a few people he will rise to power.*
>
> *— Daniel 11:23*

Antiochus IV Epiphanes came to power after Seleucus IV Philopator was assassinated by his Tax Minister, Heliodorus. The legitimate heir, Demetrius I Soter, replaced Antiochus as a hostage in Rome, and with the help of King Eumenes II of Pergamum, Antiochus IV traveled from

Athens, through Asia Minor and reached Syria by November 175 BC and seized the throne. He proclaimed himself co-regent with another son of Seleucus, an infant named Antiochus (whom he then murdered in 170 BC).[35]

> *When the richest provinces feel secure, he will invade them and will achieve what neither his fathers nor his forefathers did. He will distribute plunder, loot and wealth among his followers. He will plot the overthrow of fortresses—but only for a time.*
>
> *– Daniel 11:24*

In the Sixth Syrian War (170-168 BC) Ptolemy VI Philometor attacked the Seleucid Empire. Antiochus IV responded by building a navy (against the terms of the Peace of Apamea) and conquered Cyprus and large parts of Egypt[36] (*what neither his fathers nor his forefathers did*; the Seleucids had never previously conquered lands in Egypt).

> *With a large army he will stir up his strength and courage against the king of the South. The king of the South will wage war with a large and very powerful army, but he will not be able to stand because of the plots devised against him.*
>
> *– Daniel 11:25*

Ptolemy VI Philometor, king of the South, reigned in Egypt from 180-164 BC. As already noted, he attacked the Seleucid Empire in the Sixth Syrian War, unsuccessfully. His reign was characterized by internal conflict with his younger brother, Ptolemy VIII for control of the Ptolemaic monarchy.[37] Antiochus IV invaded Egypt in 170 BC, conquering all but Alexandria and capturing King Ptolemy.[33]

> *Those who eat from the king's provisions will try to destroy him; his army will be swept away, and many will fall in battle. The two kings, with their hearts bent on evil, will sit at the same*

table and lie to each other, but to no avail, because an end will
still come at the appointed time.

— Daniel 11:26-27

The two kings referred to in this part of the prophecy could be referring to Ptolemy VI and Antiochus IV after Antiochus captured Ptolemy. It could also refer to Ptolemy VI and Ptolemy VIII who were brothers. After Antiochus captured Ptolemy, he allowed Ptolemy VI to continue ruling as a puppet king from Memphis, to avoid alarming Rome. At that time, the city of Alexandria chose a new king, Ptolemy VIII Euergetes. Then the Ptolemy brothers agreed to rule Egypt jointly instead of fighting a civil war.[33]

The king of the North will return to his own country with great
wealth, but his heart will be set against the holy covenant. He
will take action against it and then return to his own country.

— Daniel 11:28

After Antiochus IV victory in Egypt, he returned to his own country. Then Antiochus IV harshly persecuted the Jews and in 169 B.C. Antiochus plundered the temple in Jerusalem, set up a garrison there and massacred many Jews in the city.[38]

At the appointed time he will invade the South again, but this
time the outcome will be different from what it was before.
Ships of the western coastlands will oppose him, and he will
lose heart.

— Daniel 11:29-30a

In 168 BC Antiochus IV led a second attack on Egypt but before he reached Alexandria, he received a message from the Roman Ambassador named Gaius Popillius Laenas that if he didn't leave Egypt immediately, Rome would declare war on the Seleucids. The Roman Ambassador would have travelled to Alexandria from Rome by ships from the west. Antiochus feared the Romans and chose to retreat and return to his own country, Syria.[33]

> *Then he will turn back and vent his fury against the holy covenant. He will return and show favor to those who forsake the holy covenant. His armed forces will rise up to desecrate the temple fortress and will abolish the daily sacrifice. Then they will set up the abomination that causes desolation.*
>
> *— Daniel 11:30b-31*

On the way returning to Syria, in 168 BC, Antiochus IV Epiphanes slaughtered men, women and children in Jerusalem. Maccabees 5:14 records:

> "*There were eighty thousand victims in the course of those three days, forty thousand dying by violence and as many again being sold into slavery.*"

Antiochus also set up an altar to the pagan god Zeus Olympius in the Jewish temple and sacrificed pigs on that altar.[39]

> *Those who are wise will instruct many, though for a time they will fall by the sword or be burned or captured or plundered. When they fall, they will receive a little help, and many who are not sincere will join them.*
>
> *— Daniel 11:33-34*

Those who are wise refer to the godly leaders of the Jewish resistance movement, also called the Hasidim. They did receive *a little help* when Mattathias, a Jewish priest, and his son Judas Maccabeus (Judah Maccabee) led the Maccabean Revolt against the Seleucid Empire. The Jewish holiday of Hanukkah commemorates the restoration of Jewish worship at the temple in Jerusalem in 164 BC, after Judah removed all of the statues depicting Greek gods and goddesses and purified it.[40]

Next, beginning in Daniel 11:36, Daniel prophesies about the Anti-Christ, who has yet to come. The details of Daniel 11:36 – 11:45 do not fit with what is known of Antiochus Epiphanes.[41]

Daniel's dreams revealed the major kingdoms to come after the Babylonians, and the detailed account of the period of the kingdoms after the death of Alexander the Great. These dreams show Daniel was inspired by God. Only the One True God could reveal to Daniel the history to unfold.

You may be thinking that Daniel 11 must have been written after all that history occurred. But linguistic evidence from the Dead Sea Scrolls demonstrates that the Hebrew and Aramaic chapters of Daniel were indeed written centuries earlier. The timing that these prophecies were written is identified in Daniel 10:1 as the third year of Cyrus, King of Persia, around 537 BC.

It is interesting to note that in Daniel Chapter 11, there are 37 specific prophecies from the beginning of this chapter until Daniel 11:35, from 537 BC (third year of Cyrus the Great) until 164 BC. Appendix 12 reiterates succinctly these 37 prophecies. As noted previously 37 is a number that shows up in various mathematical aspects of the scriptures, starting in Genesis 1:1 which has a gematria of 2701, which is 37 X 73.

Before moving on, I want to clarify some things in the Book of Daniel that seem to not line up with mainstream secular history, for instance that Belshazzar was not the King of the Babylonians, but is recorded in the Book of Daniel as in control when the Persians invaded Babylon. I found the article by Kyle Pope to be very helpful: "Belshazzar and Darius the Mede: Was Daniel Wrong?" (https://focusmagazine.org/belshazzar-and-darius-the-mede-was-daniel-wrong.php)

To summarize the article, Nabonidus was the last king of the Babylonians, but his son, Belshazzar was entrusted with authority of kingship in his father's absence. In Daniel 5:16, Daniel is offered the position, "third highest ruler in the kingdom" by Belshazzar if he can interpret the writing on the wall. Belshazzar offered the position of "third highest" because his father was first, he was second, and the next he could offer was third.

That very night Belshazzar, king of the Babylonians, was slain, and Darius the Mede took over the kingdom, at the age of sixty-two."

— Daniel 5:30-31

This Darius should not be confused with Darius I who ruled from 522 – 486 BC. He was the third king after Cyrus the Great and father of Xerxes. The article shows that this Darius was the son of Ahasuerus, of the lineage of the Medes, and was the last king of the Medes, known to the Greeks as Cyxares II, the son of Astyages. Darius was made ruler of the Babylonian kingdom and Cyrus was the King of Persia.

So Daniel prospered during the reign of Darius and the reign of Cyrus the Persian.

— Daniel 6:28

The Medes and Persians overlapped historically, with the Medes dying out and the Persians taking over. Esther 1:19 refers to *"the laws of the Persians and the Medes"*.

CHAPTER 11

Prophecies of Jesus' First Coming as Personal Savior of Our Sins

Christianity is founded on Jesus Christ, who came to earth as God in a physical, fleshly body, lived a perfect, blameless, sinless life. Then, He died for our sins on the cross, on the hill, Golgotha—Place of the Skull. He rose from the grave never to die again. He appeared to his disciples and more than 500 persons (1 Corinthians 15:6) at an assembly after his death on the cross and before he ascended to heaven. The four Gospels (Matthew, Mark, Luke and John) and the first chapter of Acts in the New Testament give written testimony to this synopsis.

In this chapter, I will present the major prophecies of Jesus' first coming as the "*Lamb of God who takes away the sin of the world*" (John 1:29). Jesus' first coming, as the "Lamb of God," for the purpose of redemption, payment for our sins, and reconciling us to God. Since Jesus paid the penalty for our sins, anyone who receives Jesus as the Lord of their life is forgiven of their sins, past, present and future. Adam and Eve lost relationship and fellowship with God after they sinned. Sin can be characterized as rebelling against God or disobeying God by breaking His commands so that we miss the mark and fall short of His glory, which brings separation and judgement from a holy God. Instead of the nature of love, they took on a fallen, sin-filled nature, the nature of Satan, the deceiver and the accuser.

However, Jesus Christ bought back both relationship and fellowship with God, an eternal fellowship, for those who believe and receive Jesus into their lives.

The first coming of the Messiah, Jesus Christ, is prophesied in the Old Testament Scriptures. There are also many prophecies of the promised Messiah as King over all the universe. Christians believe these prophecies will be fulfilled at the second coming of Christ. Those of the Jewish faith believe the Messiah has not yet come. They mis-understand the prophecies of the Messiah's first coming and are waiting for the Messiah's coming when he will come as King. The faithful in Christ are waiting for the Messiah's return, when He will come as reigning King of all His creation. All mankind's true enemy, the devil and demons, have done everything possible to deceive all inhabitants of the earth of the truth of Jesus Christ.

The first sin committed by human beings is recorded in Genesis 3. God told Adam they could eat of any tree in the Garden of Eden except one tree, the tree of the knowledge of good and evil. He warned ahead of time of the consequence of eating of that one tree: the consequence would be death, separation. The separation took place immediately, after Adam ate the forbidden fruit. The physical death occurred nearly a thousand years later.

When the serpent deceived Eve, she ate from the tree, and gave to Adam, her husband, and death entered the world. The great Fall of Mankind occurred. However, from the very beginning God had a plan to redeem mankind and He gives the first prophecy of the coming Messiah in Genesis 3:15 when God tells the serpent:

> *And I will put enmity between you and the woman, and between your offspring and hers; he will crush your head, and you will strike his heel.*
>
> *— Genesis 3:15*

Mankind's existence from the Fall onward has been increasingly sinful. Before the flood, described in Genesis 6-8, it got so bad that, "*The LORD saw how great man's wickedness on the earth had become, and that every inclination of the thoughts of his heart was only evil all the time."* (Genesis 6:5) From that ancient time to the present, *"All have sinned and fall short of the glory of God."* (Romans 3:23)

Satan deceived Eve to get her and Adam to disobey God. Satan most assuredly continues to act deceitfully to trick human beings into making sinful decisions, and to keep them from the knowledge of God. God's plan from the very beginning, though was to send his Son, God Himself in the flesh, to pay the penalty for mankind's sin, by dying on the cross. At this first prophecy in Genesis 3:15, *from the offspring of the woman would come One who would "crush the head" of Satan.*

Satan knew Jesus was the Son of God when He came to earth. He didn't realize though, that when he thought he successfully arranged Jesus' death on the cross that he was actually participating with God's plan of redemption. He would break the consequence of sin—death—over humankind by paying the penalty for sin Himself. Thus, Satan did strike Jesus' heel, but God crushed Satan's head. It was God's plan from the beginning to redeem mankind from the consequence of sin by paying the penalty of death Himself in our place. The only requirement for human beings is that each individual must choose to receive Jesus personally into his/her life. As written in the Gospel of John:

> *For God so loved the world that He gave His One and Only Son that whoever believes in Him shall not perish but have everlasting life.*
>
> *— John 3:16*

> *Yet to all who received him (Jesus), to those who believed in his name, he gave the right to become children of God— children born not of natural descent, nor of human decision or a husband's will, but born of God.*
>
> *— John 1:12-13*

This good news of God coming to live among us in the flesh and then dying for our sins, to pay the penalty for our sins, to be our Savior spiritually, is prophesied in the Old Testament. God coming to the earth and living among us is prophesied in Zechariah.

> *"Shout and be glad, O Daughter of Zion. For **I am coming**, and **I will live among you**," declares the LORD. "Many nations will be joined with the LORD in that day and will become my people. I will live among you and you will know that **the LORD Almighty has sent me to you.**"*
>
> *– Zechariah 2:10-11*

In this prophecy the Lord says "I" am coming and "I" will live among you. Then He says "the LORD Almighty has sent *me* to you." Jesus was God, was with God, and is the form of God we humans actually see whenever He appears to anyone on earth. The Lord Almighty sent His Son Jesus to live among us. God in the flesh.

Isaiah 7:14 is a prophecy that lets us know how God planned to come into the world as "God in the flesh".

> *Therefore the LORD himself will give you a sign: The virgin will be with child and will give birth to a son, and will call him Immanuel.*
>
> *– Isaiah 7:14*

Immanuel means "God with us". God came to earth and lived among us. The Gospels testify that Mary was a virgin when she became impregnated with Jesus, the Son of God. The Gospel of Luke describes the birth of Jesus foretold by an angel to Mary.

> *In the sixth month, God sent the angel Gabriel to Nazareth, a town in Galilee, to a virgin pledged to be married to a man named Joseph, a descendant of David. The virgin's name was*

Mary. The angel went to her and said, "Greetings, you who are highly favored! The LORD is with you." Mary was greatly trouble at his words and wondered what kind of greeting this might be. But the angel said to her, "Do not be afraid, Mary, you have found favor with God. You will be with child and give birth to a son, and you are to give him the name Jesus. He will be great and will be called the Son of the Most High. The Lord God will give him the throne of his father David, and he will reign over the house of Jacob forever; his kingdom will never end." "How will this be," Mary asked the angel, "since I am a virgin?" The angel answered, "The Holy Spirit will come upon you, and the power of the Most High will overshadow you. So the holy one to be born will be called the Son of God.

– Luke 1:26-35

Jesus in Hebrew is pronounced Yeshua, and means "salvation". When Jesus comes for the second time, He will come as king. His first coming, through the virgin Mary, was for the purpose of breaking the consequence of sin over mankind, for the spiritual salvation of mankind.

Isaiah 52:13 through the entire chapter of Isaiah 53 is a prophecy of the "servant" who will be used by God to bring spiritual salvation to mankind. This spiritual salvation is given through the death of the righteous one for the sins of mankind.

See my servant will act wisely; he will be raised and lifted up and highly exalted. Just as there were many who were appalled at him—his appearance was so disfigured beyond that of any man and his form marred beyond human likeness—so will he sprinkle many nations, and kings will shut their mouths because of him. For what they were not told, they will see, and what they have not heard, they will understand.

Who has believed our message and to whom has the arm of the LORD been revealed? He grew up before him like a tender shoot, and like a root out of dry ground. He had no beauty or majesty to attract us to him, nothing in his appearance that we should desire him. He was despised and rejected by men, a man of sorrows, and familiar with suffering. Like one from whom men hide their faces he was despised, and we esteemed him not.

Surely he took up our infirmities and carried our sorrows, yet we considered him stricken by God, smitten by him, and afflicted. But he was pierced for our transgressions, he was crushed for our iniquities; the punishment that brought us peace was upon him, and by his wounds we are healed. We all, like sheep, have gone astray, each of us has turned to his own way; and the LORD has laid on him the iniquity of us all.

He was oppressed and afflicted, yet he did not open his mouth; he was led like a lamb to the slaughter, and as a sheep before her shearers is silent, so he did not open his mouth. By oppression and judgment, he was taken away. And who can speak of his descendants? For he was cut off from the land of the living; for the transgression of my people he was stricken. He was assigned a grave with the wicked, and with the rich in his death, though he had done no violence, nor was any deceit in his mouth.

Yet it was the LORD's will to crush him and cause him to suffer, and though the LORD makes his life a guilt offering, he will see his offspring and prolong his days, and the will of the LORD will prosper in his hand. After the suffering of his soul, he will see the light of life and be satisfied; by his knowledge my righteous servant will justify many, and he will bear their iniquities. Therefore, I will give him a portion among the great, and he will divide the spoils with the strong, because he poured out his life unto death, and was numbered with the transgressors. For he bore the sin of many, and made intercession for the transgressors.

— Isaiah 52:13 – 53:12

This passage of scripture is an amazing prophecy of what Jesus accomplished on the cross, written about 700 years before Christ was born. He was physically disfigured through Roman flogging, the crown of thorns and beatings. He was killed, but *"after the suffering of his soul, he will see the light of life"* he was raised back to life. *"The punishment that brought us peace was upon him."* The righteous servant in this passage was made to be a guilt offering for the sins of mankind. And only God himself could be the perfect "lamb of God", sinless. No one else's death could be used of God to pay for the penalty of mankind's sin, only the sinless Jesus, the Righteous Suffering Servant.

This passage of scripture also gives some details of this Righteous Servant's death that happened when Jesus died. It says *"he was pierced for our transgressions"*. The soldiers broke the legs of the other men who were crucified with Jesus to hasten their death, but they did not break Jesus' legs because they saw he was already dead. *"Instead, one of the soldiers pierced Jesus' side with a spear, bringing a sudden flow of blood and water."* (John 19:34)

The passage also mentions that *"He was assigned a grave with the wicked, and with the rich in his death"*. Jesus was crucified between two criminals. But after he died, Joseph of Arimathea asked Pilate for Jesus' body and he and a pharisee named Nicodemas brought a mixture of myrrh and aloes, about seventy-five pounds, and wrapped Jesus' body with the spices, in strips of linen, according to the Jewish burial customs and placed Jesus body in a new tomb in a nearby garden (from John19:38-42). Jesus was placed in a rich man's tomb, although he died between two criminals.

David also prophesied about the crucifixion in Psalm 22. Jesus quoted Psalm 22:1 on the cross when he shouted *"My God, my God, why have you forsaken me?"* A description of Jesus at the cross is vividly portrayed in this Psalm:

> *Dogs have surrounded me; a band of evil men has encircled me; they have pierced my hands and my feet. I can count all my bones; people stare and gloat over me. They divide my garments among them and cast lots for my clothing.*
>
> *— Psalm 22:16-18*

This is an exact representation of what happened to Jesus on the cross. His hands and his feet were nailed to the cross. He was crucified naked and the soldiers cast lots for his clothing. As it is recorded in the Gospel of John:

> *When the soldiers crucified Jesus, they took his clothes, dividing them into four shares, one for each of them, with the undergarment remaining. This garment was seamless, woven in one piece from top to bottom. "Let's not tear it," they said to one another, "let's decide by lot who will get it." This happened that the scripture might be fulfilled which said, "They divided my garments among them and cast lots for my clothing." So, this is what the soldiers did.*
>
> *— John 19:23-24*

Also, Psalm 22 records a prophetic description of what the people would say who saw Jesus on the cross.

> *But I am a worm and not a man, scorned by men and despised by the people. All who see me mock me; they hurl insults, shaking their heads: "He trusts in the LORD; let the LORD rescue him. Let him deliver him, since he delights in him."*
>
> *— Psalm 22:6-8*

We see the same language recorded in Matthew 27.

> *In the same way the chief priests, the teachers of the law and the elders mocked him. "He saved others," they said, "but he can't save himself! He's the King of Israel! Let him come down now from the cross, and we will believe in him. He trusts in God. Let God rescue him now if he wants him, for he said, 'I am the Son of God.'"*
>
> *— Matthew 27:41-43*

Jesus most assuredly could have come down off the cross. He stated himself, "*Do you think I cannot call on my Father, and he will at once put at my disposal more than twelve legions of angels?*" (Matthew 26:53) But, Jesus knew his purpose was to die for the sins of mankind. He willingly chose to die on the cross. Those who mocked him thought they were doing the right thing, killing a man who blasphemed against God by calling himself the Son of God. When he did not "save himself", it further proved in their minds that they were getting rid of this "evil" person. Jesus never lied, never stole, never broke a single commandment. He healed people, raised persons from the dead, multiplied food, and calmed storms. Yet the religious elite at that time believed Jesus was guilty of the sin of blasphemy, and so he was worthy of death in their view. Jesus stated among many other things: "*Before Abraham was born, I AM*" (John 8:58). They totally missed God's plan of redemption that the Messiah would come initially as the Lamb of God to save mankind from the penalty of sin and restore a relationship between God and mankind.

Jesus fulfilled other prophecies about the coming Messiah in the Old Testament as well. The Messiah, who would be ruler over Israel, would come from the tribe of Judah, and be born in Bethlehem.

> *But you, Bethlehem Ephrathah, though you are small among the clans of Judah, out of you will come for me one who*

will be ruler over Israel, whose origins are from of old, from ancient times.

— Micah 5:2

The Gospel of Luke records Jesus' birth in Bethlehem. The lineage of Jesus from Joseph through King David's son, Solomon, is written in Matthew 1:1-17 and shows that Jesus came from the tribe of Judah, 14 generations from Abraham to David and 14 generations from King David to the exile in Babylon and 14 generations from the exile to the Messiah. Jesus' entry into the earth as a human being was divinely orchestrated by God in perfect historical timing. The lineage of Jesus from Mary's line is listed in Luke 3:23-38 and shows his lineage through David's son Nathan. Nathan is listed as one of David's sons in 2 Samuel 5:14 and 1 Chronicles 3:5. Thus, Jesus was firmly descended of David. Also, as prophesied in Micah 5:2 Jesus will be ruler over Israel. Jesus will reign from Jerusalem at His second coming.

Daniel prophesies the timing of the coming of the "Anointed One", which coincides with Jesus' life on earth and the destruction of the second Temple.

Know and understand this: From the issuing of the decree to restore and rebuild Jerusalem until the Anointed One, the ruler, comes, there will be seven 'sevens,' and sixty-two 'sevens'. … After the sixty-two 'sevens,' the Anointed One will be cut off and will have nothing. The people of the ruler who will come will destroy the city and the sanctuary.

— Daniel 9:25-26

There were four main decrees given by Cyrus, Darius, and two from Artaxerxes, Kings of Persia concerning the return of the Jews to Jerusalem and Judah, the rebuilding of the temple, and the rebuilding of the wall of Jerusalem. The first decree is recorded in Ezra 1 in the first year of Cyrus, King of Persia, 538 BC, which allowed any of the Jews to return to

Jerusalem and Judah. A second decree was issued by Darius as recorded in Ezra 6 which allowed for the completion of the building of the temple. As recorded in Ezra 6:15 "*The temple was completed on the third day of the month Adar, in the sixth year of the reign of King Darius.*" This date is equivalent to March 12, 516 B.C. Then King Artaxerxes issued a decree in 458 BC as recorded in Ezra 7, where Ezra and others returned to Jerusalem. This was the 7th year of King Artaxerxes. Then in the 20th year of King Artaxerxes, 445 BC, Nehemiah left Persia in the month of Nisan, at the decree of the king with letters of travel for safe transport in order to lead the building of the wall around Jerusalem. (Nehemiah 2:1-7)

From this last decree which completed the restoration of Jerusalem, in 445 B.C., adding 69 'sevens' or 69x7, is 483 years. But Biblical years are 360 days (lunar calendar), not 365 days. A lunar year is equal to 360 days, so 483 lunar years is equal to 483 x 360 days, or 173,880 days. Converting 173,880 days in solar years is 476.057 solar years. If you add 476 solar years to 445 BC you arrive at AD 31, precisely the time of Jesus' ministry on earth. Daniel's prophecy also declares that the "*Anointed One will be cut off*". This happened when Jesus was crucified. And then "*the ruler who will come will destroy the city and the sanctuary*". The destruction of Jerusalem happened in 70 AD when Titus also destroyed the second temple. Jesus also predicted the destruction of the second temple when he said to his disciples after they commented on the temple building: "*Do you see all these things? I tell you the truth, not one stone here will be left on another; every one will be thrown down.*" (Matthew 24:2)

Jesus also fulfilled several other prophecies written in the book of Zechariah.

Rejoice greatly, O Daughter of Zion! Shout, Daughter of Jerusalem! See, your king comes to you, righteous and having salvation, gently and riding on a donkey, on a colt, the foal of a donkey.

– Zechariah 9:9

This happened on what we now call Palm Sunday when Jesus entered Jerusalem riding on a colt with crowds of people spreading their cloaks on the road and cutting branches from trees and spreading them on the road and shouting *"Hosanna to the Son of David!" "Blessed is he who comes in the name of the Lord!"* (Matthew 21:9)

The money that Judas received for letting the Chief Priests know where they could find Jesus at night in order to arrest him secretively is also prophesied in Zechariah:

> *I told them, "If you think it best, give me my pay; but if not, keep it." So they paid me thirty pieces of silver. And the LORD said to me, "Throw it to the potter"—the handsome price at which they priced me! So I took the thirty pieces of silver and threw them into the house of the LORD to the potter.*
>
> *– Zechariah 11:12-13*

Matthew records that *"Judas Iscariot went to the chief priests and asked, 'What are you willing to give me if I hand him over to you?' So they counted out for him thirty silver coins."* (Matthew 26:14-15) Then, later in Matthew 27, Judas regrets what he had done. He says to the chief priests:

> *"I have sinned, for I have betrayed innocent blood." "What is that to us?" they replied. "That's your responsibility." So Judas threw the money into the temple and left. Then he went away and hanged himself. The chief priests picked up the coins and said, "It is against the law to put this into the treasury, since it is blood money." So they decided to use the money to buy the potter's field as a burial place for foreigners.*
>
> *– Matthew 27:4-7*

Also, in Zechariah is the prophecy that the inhabitants of Jerusalem will look on "me", the LORD speaking, whom they have pierced.

*And I will pour out on the house of David and the inhabitants of Jerusalem a spirit of grace and supplication. They will look on **me**, the one they have pierced, and they will mourn for **him** as one mourns for an only child, and grieve bitterly for him as one grieves for a firstborn son.*

– Zechariah 12:10

It is God's tremendous act of grace that He paid the penalty for our sins. In this prophecy the pronouns change from "me" to "him". God's one and only Son was the one who was pierced when He was crucified in Jerusalem. These prophecies from Genesis, Psalms, Isaiah, Daniel, Micah, and Zechariah reveal the timing of the Messiah's coming, the method through a virgin birth, the place of birth, the lineage from King David, the purpose of the Messiah's first coming to die for the sins of mankind, entering Jerusalem on a colt with the praises of the people, the amount of betrayal blood money and what it would be used for, the suffering and type of death the Messiah would endure, specifics about what people would say about him while on the cross, the casting of lots for his clothes, and specifics about his burial. And this isn't even a comprehensive list!

Jesus fulfilled the prophecies about the Righteous Servant, the Suffering Servant, and the Savior of the world, who would serve as a guilt offering for the sins of the world. This is the Promised Messiah, Jesus. I won't go into the prophecies about the second coming of Jesus, since they have not yet been fulfilled. But we are VERY close to His second coming when Jesus will restore all things and become King over the whole earth, ruling from Jerusalem.

I urge you to receive Jesus as your Savior. He died for your sins so that you can have eternal life. Ask Him right now to come into your life. He will forgive your sins, come into your life, and make you a new creation. As it says in 2 Corinthians 5:17 "*Therefore, if anyone is in Christ, he is a new creation; the old has gone, the new has come!*"

CHAPTER 12

Return of Jews to Israel

Another amazing prophecy of scripture is the return of Jewish people to their Promised Land in Israel after over 2000 years from being scattered to nations all over the earth. The Jews returned to Jerusalem and the southern kingdom of Judah from Babylon 70 years after the Babylonian captivity beginning in 538 BC. The 10 tribes of the northern kingdom of Israel that fell to the Assyrians, prior to the Babylonian Captivity, never returned. And after the time of Christ and the destruction of Jerusalem in 70 AD, the Jews that lived in the Roman-occupied land of Israel were scattered all over the earth. It is a miracle that the Jewish people remained a distinct people group over the last 2000 years and that they received back their land becoming once again the nation of Israel in 1948 from the United Nations resolution. Before looking at these prophecies, it's important to know how Israel became a nation in the first place. As recorded in Genesis 12:1 God spoke to a man named Abram and called him to leave his country and *"go to the land I will show you."* He told Abram:

> *I will make you into a **great nation** and I will bless you; I will make your name great, and you will be a blessing. I will bless those who bless you, and whoever curses you I will curse; and **all peoples on earth will be blessed through you.***
>
> *— Genesis 12:2-3*

When Abram was 99 years old God changed his name to Abraham (Gen 17:5) and his wife's name Sarai to Sarah (Gen 17:15) and told them that Sarah would give birth to a son. Sarah gave birth to Isaac when Abraham was 100 and she was 90. This was a miraculous birth, as all conceptions and births are, however this birth was part of God's promise and prophecy that from the woman's seed would come one who would crush the head of satan from Genesis 3:15. Isaac was not the promised Messiah, but from his lineage eventually Jesus Christ would be born. When Jesus Christ bore the sin of mankind on the cross, he offered salvation from sins to all who would receive Him. Indeed *"all peoples on earth will be blessed through you"*, through the seed of Abraham, through Jesus Christ.

It is interesting to take a closer look at Isaac's name in Hebrew which shows in the four letters of Isaac's name, the second letter, Tsadi, is equivalent to 90 and the last letter, *Kof,* is equivalent to 100, corresponding to Sarah's age and Abraham's age when Isaac was born.

יִצְחָק   Isaac's name in Hebrew

Isaac's miraculous birth and his name were ordained and designed by God through His sovereign will. It was part of His plan to make a chosen people from whom He would work out His plan of salvation through Jesus Christ. And God foreshadowed Jesus' death when He called Abraham to sacrifice Isaac, and then provided a ram as recorded in Genesis 22. Eventually God provided His One and Only Son to be the sacrificial lamb who would provide both forgiveness of sin and just payment of sin.

Moving along to the formation of the nation Israel, Isaac married Rebekah and she gave birth to twins, Jacob and Esau. Jacob had 12 sons, and God changed Jacob's name to Israel (Gen 32:28). His 12 sons became the 12 tribes of Israel. One of his sons, Joseph, was sold into slavery by his brothers and went to Egypt, where God providentially brought Joseph from prison to palace and made him leader of all Egypt just under Pharaoh. Eventually because of a great famine, Jacob and his 11 other sons and his whole family (70 in all) moved to Egypt and were reunited with Joseph.

After about 400 years in Egypt, Jacob's initial 70 had grown to nearly 2 million people and were treated harshly as slaves in Egypt. The Israelites left Egypt under the leadership of Moses after God caused ten severe plagues in Egypt when Pharaoh refused to let the Israelites leave Egypt. The Israelites were to return to the Promised Land, but they rebelled against Moses and didn't trust God, so they wandered in the desert for 40 years.

Eventually Joshua led the Israelites back into the Promised Land sometime around 1406 B.C., or possibly as late as 1250 B.C. Israel was ruled by Judges until the monarchy when Saul was anointed as the first King (1 Samuel 10:1) in 1050 B.C. The first temple was built during Solomon's reign in 960 B.C. Thus, Israel was a nation beginning in 1050 B.C., about 3070 years ago, with Saul as the first King, or several hundred years before that when Israel was ruled by God through the Judges.

Israel split into the Northern Kingdom of Israel (10 tribes) and the Southern Kingdom of Judah (2 tribes) at the end of Solomon's reign in 930 B.C. The Northern Kingdom was destroyed by the Assyrians and many Israelites were taken to Assyria from about 745 – 705 B.C. So, the Northern Kingdom of Israel ceased to be a nation by 705 B.C.

The Babylonians attacked the Southern Kingdom of Judah, or Judea, beginning in 597 B.C. when thousands were deported to the Babylonian empire. Jerusalem and Solomon's Temple were destroyed in 586 B.C. with a second deportation of Jews to Babylon.

The Jews who were deported to Babylon were allowed to return to Judah after 70 years of captivity. They completed building the Second Temple in 516 B.C. and they rebuilt the Wall around Jerusalem between 445-425 BC. The Jews living there were under control of the Greeks—the Ptolemaic and Seleucid Dynasty's from 332-141 BC, and the Hasmonean Dynasty beginning in 141 BC. The Roman General Pompey captured Jerusalem in 63 BC, and the Roman forces destroyed Jerusalem and demolished the Second Temple in 70 AD. Jerusalem was rebuilt as a Roman City and the Romans renamed the area of Judea to Filistia (Palestine) in 135 AD.

To complete the history to the present time, the land of Israel (Palestine) was ruled by Byzantine Christians from 324 – 638 AD. Then the first Muslim period was from 638 – 1099 AD. The Dome of the Rock was built near the site of the destroyed Jewish Temples in 691 AD. The Crusader Period was from 1099-1187 AD, the Ayyubid Period from 1187-1259 AD, the Muslim Mamluk Period from 1250-1516 AD, The Turkish Ottoman Empire from 1516-1917, and under British rule from 1917-1948.

On Friday, May 14, 1948 Israel became a nation once again under the November 29, 1947 resolution of the United Nations. Palestine was to be partitioned between Arabs and Jews allowing for the formation of the Jewish state of Israel. At the birth of the new nation, the population in Israel was 872,700. Previous to May 14, 1948, the region of Palestine (Palestine was never a nation) was ruled by the British and both Jewish and Arab people lived in the region.

The United Nations made this resolution because of the 6 million⁺ Jews who were annihilated in Europe and the huge humanitarian crisis for the survivors who had no homes, no jobs, very sick, and destitute. It was decided that these refugees could be sent to the new nation of Israel. The Jews were very happy for this arrangement, but the Arabs were not.

No one living in Palestine was to be displaced when Israel became a nation. But on the eve of Friday, May 14, 1948, the first day that Israel was officially a nation according to the United Nations, five Arab countries— Lebanon, Syria, Iraq, Egypt and Saudi Arabia—attacked the infant nation by launching an air attack on Tel Aviv and invaded the new nation. The Arab nations warned the Arabs living there of the attack and many of them left the area temporarily thinking that the Arab attack would be successful and then they would move back. *Miraculously*, however, Israel survived and Israel and the Arab states reached an armistice agreement in February 1949.

Then on June 5, 1967 Israel's neighboring countries of Egypt, Jordan and Syria attacked Israel. This Six-Day War ended on June 10, 1967 with Israel capturing the Sinai Peninsula, the Golan Heights, the Gaza Strip, and the West Bank, including East Jerusalem.

As of 2020, Israel has a population of 8.7 million (worldpopulation-review.com). Although it is considered a Jewish state, it is a parliamentary democracy, with freedom of religion and roughly 21% of the citizens are Arabs. The Jewish, Muslim, and Christian citizens living in Israel are living peacefully, however terrorism from various groups outside of Israel, insisting that Israel is Palestine, continues. It is interesting to note that Israel has an area of 10,762 square miles (post 1967 borders), which is less than 1% of the total land area of the Arab-controlled countries in the Middle East. Its land mass is comparable to New Jersey, the 5th smallest US state.

Summarizing this background of ancient and present-day Israel, it is noteworthy that Israel became a nation again after over 2500 years of ceasing to exist as a nation. And this phenomenon is thoroughly prophesied in the Old Testament.

We will look at several of these prophecies, but before that, I want to point out another interesting fact concerning Abraham and the year 1948 when Israel became a nation again. Since the ages and births of Abraham's ancestors are recorded in the Bible from Adam through to Abraham, it is possible to discover exactly how many years existed from Adam's creation to Abraham's birth. Want to guess how many years? One Thousand Nine Hundred and Forty Eight (1948). Abraham was born 1948 years after Adam was created. Abraham was the father of the promised nation, Israel, and after Jesus Christ was born, Israel became a nation again in 1948. Table 1 below shows the details from Adam to Abram, later renamed Abraham. Abraham was the 20th generation from Adam.

Table 1. Lineage from Adam to Abram

Year of Birth	Name	Generation	Age at birth of son	Additional years after birth of son	Years lived	Year of death	Scripture Reference
0	Adam	1	130	800	930	930	Genesis 5:3-5
130	Seth	2	105	807	912	1042	Genesis 5:6-8
235	Enosh	3	90	815	905	1140	Genesis 5:9-11
325	Kenan	4	70	840	910	1235	Genesis 5:12-14
395	Mahalalel	5	65	830	895	1290	Genesis 5:15-17
460	Jared	6	162	800	962	1422	Genesis 5:18-20
622	Enoch	7	65	300	365	987	Genesis 5:21-24
687	Methuselah	8	187	782	969	1656	Genesis 5:25-27
874	Lamech	9	182	595	777	1651	Genesis 5:28-31
1056	Noah	10	500	450	950	2006	Gen 5:32, Gen 9:29
1556	Shem (Ham, Japeth)	11	102	500	600	2156	Gen 11:10-11
1658	Arphaxad	12	35	403	438	2096	Gen 11:12-13
1693	Shelah	13	30	403	433	2126	Gen 11:14-15
1723	Eber	14	34	430	464	2187	Gen 11:16-17
1757	Peleg	15	30	209	239	1996	Gen 11:18-19
1787	Reu	16	32	207	239	2026	Gen 11:20-21
1819	Serug	17	30	200	230	2049	Gen 11:22-23
1849	Nahor	18	29	119	148	1997	Gen 11:24-25
1878	Terah	19	70	135	205	2083	Gen 11:26, 32
1948	Abram (Nahor, Haran)	20	100	75	175	2123	Gen 21:5, Gen 25:7

When I visited Israel in the Fall of 2018, one of the places I visited was the Alijah Return Center. "Alijah" is the Hebrew word which refers to Jewish persons returning home to their Promised Land in Israel from the nations where they have been scattered. According to reformjudaism.org, the "First Aliyah" occurred in the late 1800's consisting mainly of persons from Russia and Yemen. And ever since then Jews have been returning to the land of Israel, especially after it became a nation in 1948. The Alijah Return Center is a place where immigrants to Israel can go who don't have a place to live or a job while they get settled into Israel. Jews from at least 52 different nations have come to this center in recent years. At this center I picked up a one-page pamphlet that shows the 64 "Aliyah" scriptures that prophesy the return of Jews to Israel from all over the world. I will include in this chapter what I consider the top ten of these "Aliyah" prophetic scriptures.

1) The first place in the Old Testament where it is prophesied that God would bring the Israelites back to Israel after scattering them all over the earth is in Deuteronomy.

*When all these blessings and curses I have set before you come upon you and you take them to heart wherever the LORD your God disperses you among the nations, and when you and your children return to the LORD your God and obey him with all your heart and with all your soul according to everything I command you today, then the LORD your God will restore your fortunes and have compassion on you and **gather you again from all the nations where he scattered you. Even if you have been banished to the most distant land under the heavens, from there the LORD your God will gather you and bring you back. He will bring you to the land that belonged to your fathers, and you will take possession of it.** He will make you more prosperous and numerous than your fathers.*

— Deuteronomy 30:1-5

These words in Deuteronomy were written by Moses about 3300 years ago, just before the Israelites returned to Israel from their captivity in Egypt. Moses warns them of blessings for obedience and curses for disobedience, but states that if they do get scattered over all the earth because of future disobedience, God will bring them back again to the promised land of Israel.

2) Isaiah prophesies about 2700 years ago that both Israel (the Northern Kingdom) and Judah (the Southern Kingdom) will return to the land of Israel after being scattered all over the earth.

*He will raise a banner for the nations and gather the exiles of **Israel**; he will assemble the scattered people of **Judah** from the four quarters of the earth.*

— Isaiah 11:12

Judah went into exile into Babylon and returned after 70 years. They again were scattered after the destruction of the second temple in 70 AD. But this prophecy in Isaiah refers to exiles of Israel, who never returned to Israel after they were taken into captivity by the Assyrians, as well as exiles from Judah. In this prophecy, it is not referring to return from Babylon, but return from being scattered all over the earth.

3) Jeremiah also prophesies about 2600 years ago of the restoration of the Israelites to the land of their forefathers after being scattered over all the earth.

> *"However, the days are coming," declares the LORD, "when men will no longer say, 'As surely as the LORD lives, who brought the Israelites up out of Egypt,' but they will say, 'As surely as the LORD lives, who brought the Israelites up out of the land of the north **and out of all the countries where he had banished them.' For I will restore them to the land I gave their forefathers.**"*

> *— Jeremiah 16:14-15*

4) Jeremiah prophesies again for both Israel and Judah that they will return to the land of Israel.

> *This is the word that came to Jeremiah from the LORD: 'This is what the LORD, the God of Israel, says: "Write in a book all the words I have spoken to you. The days are coming", declares the LORD, "when **I will bring my people Israel and Judah back from captivity and restore them to the land I gave their forefathers to possess"** says the LORD.*

> *— Jeremiah 30:1-3*

5) The LORD gave Ezekiel the same message when Ezekiel prophesied about 2600 years ago:

> *Therefore say: 'This is what the Sovereign LORD says: "**I will gather you from the nations and bring you back from the**"*

countries where you have been scattered, and I will give you back the land of Israel again.'"

– Ezekiel 11:17

6) Ezekiel expands the prophecy later with this account:

This is what the Sovereign LORD says: **"When I gather the people of Israel from the nations where they have been scattered, I will show myself holy among them in the sight of the nations.** *Then they will live in their own land, which I gave to my servant Jacob.* **They will live there in safety and will build houses and plant vineyards;** *they will live in safety when I inflict punishment on all their neighbors who maligned them. Then they will know that I am the LORD their God."*

– Ezekiel 28:25-26

It seems like Israel is in the news constantly after being bombed, fires started by kites, acts of terrorism, threats of annihilation. However, Israel is growing in population, houses are being built, and much of the former wasteland is now producing crops. Israel produces 95% of its own food, is a major exporter of fresh produce, and a world leader in agricultural technologies. The Iron Dome keeps most missiles from landing in Israel. When I visited Israel in 2018, I felt quite safe, and persons who I talked with who live there feel safe despite the constant attacks against their country.

7) In this prophecy from Ezekiel, there is mention of a period of darkness before the LORD brings them back to the land of Israel from all over the world. The Holocaust was the catalyst that caused the UN resolution to create the nation of Israel in 1948.

For this is what the Sovereign LORD says: "I myself will search for my sheep and look after them. As a shepherd looks after his scattered flock when he is with them, so will I look after my sheep. **I will rescue them from all the places where they were scattered on a day of clouds and darkness. I will bring them out from the nations and gather them from the countries, and I will bring them into their own land.** *I will pasture them on the mountains of Israel, in the ravines and in all the settlements in the land. ..."*

— Ezekiel 34:11-13

8) In this prophecy from Ezekiel, there is an additional prophecy about the spiritual renewal of Israel, not just the physical renewal of the country.

"For I will take you out of the nations; I will gather you from all the countries and bring you back into your own land. I will sprinkle clean water on you, and you will be clean; I will cleanse you from all your impurities and from all your idols. **I will give you a new heart and put a new spirit in you;** *I will remove from you your heart of stone and give you a heart of flesh. And* **I will put my Spirit in you** *and move you to follow my decrees and be careful to keep my laws. You will live in the land I gave your forefathers; you will be my people, and I will be your God."*

— Ezekiel 36:24-28

God says he will give them a new heart and put a new spirit in them. This is the same thing he has done for the gentiles who have received Jesus as their Lord and Savior. Jesus died for our sins and whoever receives Jesus into their lives is born again. The Holy Spirit comes and lives inside the new believer making each one into a new creation. An increasing number of Jewish people are coming to realize that Jesus is the Messiah, that Yeshua is the Mashiach. They are not converting to Christianity, they stay Jewish, but they become Messianic Jews: Jews who believe that Jesus is the Messiah. They still believe Jesus will return again as King, but it will be his second coming, not his first.

9) Again, Ezekiel prophesies the return to the land and the pouring out of God's Spirit on the people in Israel.

> *Therefore, this is what the Sovereign LORD says: "I will now bring Jacob back from captivity and will have compassion on all the people of Israel, and I will be zealous for my holy name. They will forget their shame and all the unfaithfulness they showed toward me when they lived in safety in their land with no one to make them afraid.* **When I have brought them back from the nations and have gathered them from the countries of their enemies,** *I will show myself holy through them in the sight of many nations. Then they will know that I am the LORD their God, for though I sent them into exile among the nations, I will gather them to their own land, not leaving any behind. I will no longer hide my face from them,* **for I will pour out my Spirit on the house of Israel,** *declares the Sovereign LORD."*
>
> — *Ezekiel 39:25-29*

This prophecy is in progress. God has brought back the Jewish people to Israel and is continuing to do so. Some Jews have received the Spirit of the Lord, the indwelling of the Holy Spirit, when they have received Jesus into their lives as their Savior and become Messianic Jews. We can expect many more Jews to come to the understanding that Jesus is the Messiah in the near future.

10) And the last scripture I'm sharing about the amazing occurrence of Israel becoming a nation again after about 2400 years is from Amos.

> *I will bring back my exiled people Israel; they will rebuild the ruined cities and live in them. They will plant vineyards and drink their wine; they will make gardens and eat their fruit.*
>
> — *Amos 9:14*

The miracle of Israel becoming a nation again after thousands of years is unique. Nothing similar has happened in history to any other nation. The fact that it is so clearly prophesied in the Bible gives solid evidence the Bible is inspired by God.

SECTION 3

THE EVIDENCE OF MIRACLES AND PERONAL TESTIMONY

CHAPTER 13

Evidence of Miracles

Some discount the Bible as not being true because of the miracles recorded in many places in the Bible. It is not possible to feed 5000+ people with five loaves and two fish, it is not possible to walk on water, it is not possible to be raised from the dead or to be miraculously healed. So, for some, the written accounts of these kind of miracles are assumed to be false claims. It is true that in the natural world the miraculous is not possible. But the Bible makes it clear that there is an invisible supernatural world. *"All things are possible with God."* (Mark 10:27)

In this section, I'd like to look at modern-day documented miracles to show that indeed miracles do happen and are available for examination today. If the miraculous happens today, then it gives evidence that the accounts written in the Bible could also have actually happened just as written.

The Christian Broadcasting Network regularly documents modern day miracles to prove that God is real. Thousands of documented miraculous healings are recorded at www.godisreal.today/modern-day-miracles.

Sid Roth has a TV show, *It's Supernatural*, with hundreds of guests who he has interviewed who have experienced supernatural miracles in their lives (see www.sidroth.org).

The Elijah Challenge has trained disciples to share the gospel, heal the sick and drive out demons as evidence that Jesus is the Messiah in over 50 countries around the world. Tens of thousands of people have been healed miraculously in the name of Jesus over the last 20 years through disciples trained through this ministry. Their website www.theelijahchallenge.org documents hundreds of supernatural healings. One such miracle documents a dead woman who was raised back to life.[1]

Lee Strobel's *The Case For Miracles*, documents scientific studies about prayer for healing, miraculous healings documented in peer-reviewed medical journals, and modern-day miracles all over the world. I will expand on a few documented miracles in this chapter.

Bruce Van Netta was nearly cut in two on November 16, 2006 when a 10,000 lb truck axle fell on him like a blunt guillotine across his mid-section crushing him to less than an inch. The accident crushed his ribs, vertebrae, pancreas, spleen, digestive intestines and completely severed five major arteries. There is no known person besides Bruce who has ever survived the severing of five major arteries. He should have bled to death in just a few minutes.

He called out "Lord help me!" Instantly all of the pain left Bruce's body, his spirit left his body and he was looking on the accident scene from above and saw two big angels with bright lights on either side of his body. He felt no pain and unspeakable peace. He realized he had a choice: 1) a very loud voice saying "shut your eyes, give up and die and go to heaven" or 2) a much quieter voice whispering, "if you want to live you are going to have to fight and it's going to be a hard fight".

The next thing he knew his spirit went back into his body. He was life-flighted to a nearby hospital. Doctors did not expect him to survive the next few hours. However, he stayed in the hospital for over two months and survived five major surgeries. Since almost 75% of his small intestines were crushed in the accident, he didn't have the ability to digest food properly and he was expected to starve to death within less than a year. He lost weight from 180 lbs to 126 lbs. even though he was being fed intravenously.

His family and friends kept on praying for Bruce and one day a man from New York who heard about the accident and had met Bruce one time previously came to visit Bruce in the hospital after having dreamt about him two days in a row. He prayed, "small intestine I command you to supernaturally grow back in the name of Jesus Christ." Bruce felt he was healed instantly. Subsequent tests showed his intestines doubled in length to nine feet and were functioning better than normal. His pancreas rejuvenated by itself, his spleen rejuvenated by itself. His total hospital stay was over nine months, but he is completely healed today. You can view his testimony on YouTube, look for "Angels Help Man Who Had a 10000 lb Truck Axle Fall – Bruce Van Netta" or read about his testimony in his book *Saved by Angels.*

Heidi and Roland Baker founded Iris Ministries (www.irisglobal.org) and have ministered 23 years and ongoing in Mozambique, the poorest country in the world. They provide orphanages for over 2,000 children in Mozambique. They have seen food multiplied, the sick healed and more than 100 people raised from the dead. Heidi has written a book, *Compelled By Love*, and documents how they *have to have miracles* in order to survive. You can view some of the stories of these miracles at www.godisreal.today/modern-day-miracles and sidroth.org TV archives of Heidi Baker interview on June 17, 2018.

I was amazed to hear the story of Josiah Cullen on March 26, 2017 when Tahni Cullen, Josiah's mother, was interviewed by Sid Roth on the TV Show *It's Supernatural.* Josiah was diagnosed as severely autistic at two years of age. By the time he was seven years old, he was still non-verbal but his mom was able to communicate through an iPad and "rapid prompting method" for about a year.

One day she read Josiah a story about when Jesus healed the blind man. She asked Josiah, "What did Jesus do? Did he H-E-A-L the blind man or P-L-A-Y with the blind man?" Josiah tapped appropriately on the "heal" letters. Then his mom was trying to help him spell h-e-a-l. He tapped on "G" and his mom thought he wasn't understanding the letters correctly. Then he touched "O", and then he went on to spell his first independent sentence: "God is a good gift giver." He had never spelled a word in his life. But from that day forward he was able to communicate through typing words on his iPad.

He revealed that Jesus taught him to read by teaching him the order of sounds and that at night he would get taken up in the spirit into heaven to go to school and was taught by an angel named Nathan. He knew things from science, history and theological concepts. He explained "Faith is picture it done." He explained profound sentences about the Trinity.

At a mall he typed to his mom that he needed to talk to a nice girl. He typed to her that this girl needed to hear the words: "...love is born out of choosing God, not Wicca". When a group of about 20 girls came nearby, Tahni reached out to one of the girls with a black cape on and said "I think I have a word for you". She told her everything her son had typed out. Another girl in the group stepped up and said that word is for me. She said "I'm in Wicca and I have been told I have daddy issues, and I just got so hot as you were saying that." You can read much more about this miraculous situation from the book by Tahni Cullen, *Josiah's Fire*.

On October 4, 2015 Samuel Rodriguez shared his testimony at Gateway Church about his experience preaching in Pakistan. There was a large audience in Pakistan with at least 60% in attendance Muslim. At one point in his sermon, he pointed to the crowd on his right and said "Jesus saves", then he pointed to the crowd in the middle and said "Jesus delivers", then he pointed to the crowd on his left and said "Jesus heals".

Sitting on the front row on his left were a group of Muslim clerics and after Samuel said "Jesus heals", there was a disturbance in the front row and two men, an 80-year-old man and his son, started yelling and approached the stage. The 80-year-old man was the lead cleric of the Muslim leaders sitting in the front row. He was born completely blind, but at the moment Samuel declared "Jesus heals" this man got healed of his blindness. He and his son came up to the stage to give testimony of his healing in the name of Jesus. You can hear this testimony on YouTube by searching for "Samuel Rodriguez The Miracle in Pakistan".

Don Piper was in a head-on automobile accident January 25, 1989 and died and went to heaven. But 90 minutes later he came back to life on earth. When the ambulance first arrived, they checked on Don and found no pulse and left him as dead. The car he was in was so destroyed, that his body was trapped in the vehicle wreckage. Miraculously, 90 minutes after the accident a bystander felt led to pray for Don and he came back to life. It took several hours to pry him out of the vehicle, but he survived and has written about his experience in heaven in his book, "*90 Minutes in Heaven.*"

Another book and movie, *Heaven is For Real,* is about how 3-year-old Colton Burpo was nearly decapitated in a car accident, but survived. He later tells of his experiences in heaven including seeing his sister, who had been a miscarriage before Colton was born, and his grandpa who looked younger than when he died. The 2010 New York Times Best Seller documents the near-death experience.

The miracles in Don Piper's life and Colton Burpo's life got a lot of press and publicity, but miracles are happening around the world on a daily basis. I receive reports from different ministries around the world with daily and weekly miracles being reported: miraculous healings, persons being raised from the dead. Miracles are happening and increasing in the days that we currently live in. They are happening now, at the soon return of Jesus Christ, just as they happened as recorded in the Bible. God is for real! And the Bible is His written Word and Revelation to us, our connection to our Creator.

CHAPTER 14

The Evidence of Personal Revelation

In this chapter, I'm going to testify how I have experienced God and heard from God through His Word and other means through the course of my life. Reflecting on my life and all the ways God has revealed Himself to me brought me to tears as I realized all the different ways that I have experienced God's personal touch in my life. God didn't just create us and then step back, hands off, and let the "experiment" run its course. God created us to be in a personal relationship with each of us. He cares for and loves each one of us deeply.

As I share these personal things about my life, the goal of these testimonies is to highlight God, not myself. I share them because they happened to me, they are part of my life story. I pray they may be an encouragement to you as well. And they also reveal God's Word to be true, interwoven in the fabric of my life.

The Evidence of Divine intervention

One of the ways God communicates to us is through divine intervention. The first experience that I recognized God's interaction in my life was when I was 14 years old in 9th grade. My family moved to Texas from

California during my 9th grade year. I was beginning to think more about God and it finally clicked in my mind that the Bible is a book about God. An English teacher made reference to the Bible in class and it struck me that she was an educated person who believed in the Bible.

I had heard the story about Adam and Eve and thought that it was a "story", kind of like Santa Claus living at the North Pole. Yet, it intrigued me that this "educated" person believed in the Bible and that the Bible was a book about God. I wasn't sure if I believed in God or not at that time, but I wished I had a Bible. I never said anything, but I definitely had the thought: "I wish I had a Bible".

A few days after that thought, my dad came home from work and asked me if I would like this Bible that someone at work gave him. He didn't like to read and he knew I was a reader and asked me if I wanted it. I said "YES" and that "coincidence" got my attention.

However, I don't believe it was mere coincidence or luck, it was divine intervention. The LORD orchestrated me getting His Word after I sincerely wished I had a Bible. It wasn't chance that someone at my dad's work gave him a Bible. That person was moved by the Holy Spirit to give my Dad a Bible, and then, God knew, he would give it to me.

Another divine intervention that stands out is my "chance" meeting with a friend, Katherine Hines, in Houston, Texas. I met Katherine at Bear Valley Church in the Denver area before I was married. We were friends, but after I got married and moved to Houston, we lost touch.

About three years passed when we ran into each other unexpectedly in Houston. She was in Houston for a business meeting with the accounting firm she worked for. I had just parked and was walking to the downtown post office to mail a tax return after 5 p.m. that needed to be postmarked that day. As I was walking across the street, I heard the honk of a car. It was Katherine. She was getting off work in her rental car and noticed me walking across the street. We reconnected.

Shortly after that, she quit her job and became a full-time missionary in Uganda. Since we were reconnected, I was able to help support her financially and prayerfully all these 25+ years because of that divine intervention on the streets of Houston.

So, is it divine intervention or coincidence? What does the Bible say about coincidences? The word "coincidence" is used one time in the New Testament by Jesus when he tells the parable of the Good Samaritan. In Luke 10:31 Jesus says *"And by a coincidence a certain priest was going on that road, and seeing him, he passed on the opposite side."* (The Interlinear Bible) The Greek word for coincidence is *sugkurian* (4795 in Strong's Exhaustive Concordance of the Bible) and is made up of two root words *sun* (4862) which means together with and *kurios* (2962) which means supreme in authority; controller; God, Lord, master, sir. Combining these two root meanings a good definition of the Biblical use of "coincidental" is "occurring together with God's controlling arrangement of circumstances".

What was going on in the spiritual world to get Katherine and I to cross paths at the exact same time on the streets of Houston and for Katherine to recognize me? God knew He wanted us to reconnect. He knew Katherine's destiny included helping children and widows in Uganda and he knew that I would be a faithful supporter of her ministry. He brought us together not by chance, but by His controlling of circumstances. We are not puppets in His hand; we have free will, but God still can orchestrate circumstances in our lives to move us along in the path that He created and planned for each one of us.

Another incident that stands out with the hand of God all over it was the first overseas trip that I ever took with my work as a Geophysicist with Schlumberger to Jakarta, Indonesia. At that time a new software was being developed called "IESX". The software was an updated version of the Interactive Exploration System that allowed geophysicists to interpret 2D and 3D seismic data. I was tasked with creating the documentation and training course for IESX and the first course I was to teach was going to be in Jakarta.

At that time, personally, I had recently finished the workbook by Henry Blackaby, *Experiencing God*. I was very excited about this oversees trip and I researched in advance if I could attend a church service while I was there. I was arriving on a Saturday and would be there for 2 weeks, so I had two Sundays in Jakarta and wanted to connect with some other Christians while there. I also asked God what I could do to be a blessing to the people I would meet and He gave me the idea to bring some *Experiencing God* workbooks with me. So, I packed a dozen *Experiencing God* workbooks with me, and I took a cab to the church I had researched that first Sunday morning. No one was expecting me.

When I arrived, there were two people at the door who greeted me. One was a lady who got wide-eyed when she noticed the *Experiencing God* workbooks I was holding. I told her I brought them to give away to bless others. She told me that she was in a group of people from the church who heard about the study and wanted to do it and were planning to order the workbooks and have them shipped to Jakarta, but were running into some problems. She was THRILLED that I gave her these books. And I was overwhelmingly happy to give them to her!

Incidentally, I met several people that day who invited me to have dinner in their homes. During my 2-week stay in Jakarta I got to eat meals with several families. My first business trip turned out to be successful as well as a wonderful personal experience. The course I taught in Jakarta for the first time became the documentation and course material that was used to teach thousands in the US, Canada, UK, China, Europe, and other places in the world how to use this technical software.

This experience in Jakarta highlights to me God's ability to bring circumstances together for His glory and blessing. It also highlights how peaceful, joyful and wonderful life is walking with God, obeying Him and seeking to advance His Kingdom. Work is joyful. It may be challenging at times. Work can be hard. But I experienced the peace and satisfaction of working hard on a secular task, but in a restful, not overly stressful way. Jesus put it this way:

> *Come to me, all you who are weary and burdened, and I will give you rest. Take my yoke upon you and learn from me, for I am gentle and humble in heart, and you will find rest for your souls. For my yoke is easy and my burden is light."*
>
> *– Matthew 11:28-30*

When we are walking with the Lord, and asking Him to use us to bless others, He just makes it all come together without burdensome effort.

Personal Word from God through the Bible

There are two Greek words for the "word" of God in the Bible, logos and rhema. Logos refers to the total inspired Word of God. One example scripture is Hebrews 4:12a *"For the word (logos) of God is living and active."* Rhema refers to a word that applies specifically to an individual's life. Typically, it's a word that when reading the Bible, it jumps out at you. You know God is speaking to you directly. I have a habit of dating scripture in my Bible when I have experienced a significant "rhema" word from God. Usually I experience "rhema" words from God on a regular, practically daily basis because I read the Bible daily. But I'd like to share two experiences that were milestones in my life.

When I was in graduate school at Texas A&M University, I went through a period of strong focus on prayer. Colossians 4:2 says *"Devote yourself to prayer being watchful and thankful."* I had an extremely busy schedule toward the end of one semester and I had finals, projects and everything due at the same time. I didn't want to waste the semester by getting low grades because I couldn't get all the final assignments and tests done. So that last week of school I got about eight hours of sleep total for the week. I worked as hard as I have ever worked. But I still spent at least an hour every day in prayer. In fact, my time in prayer, more than sleep, sustained me during the week. I made it through the week and I remember after crashing and waking up I had no idea if it was morning or evening or what day it was. But I realized I had not personally read from the Bible in weeks, maybe months.

With school work behind me for the semester I popped open my Bible, placed my finger on a verse and started reading. Psalm 119:16b *"I will not neglect your word."* The LORD spoke to me definitively, directly, and strongly. I had definitely neglected His word. In my busyness I got to the point that I didn't even bother to open up the Bible. Thankfully, the LORD got my attention early in my adult life that daily Bible reading is essential for a healthy spiritual life. Jesus said in Matthew 4:4 *"Man does not live on bread alone, but on every word (rhema) that comes from the mouth of God."*

Another rhema word that I'd like to share was in the summer during Graduate School. I had taken the spring semester off of school in order to work and save money, and then I went to Minnesota on a summer missions trip through the Baptist Student Union. So, I took a break from graduate school for about six months. At the end of that time, my husband, Ted, proposed to me. I decided to marry him, and planned to quit graduate school. But one week before the Fall semester was to begin at Texas A & M, I got a rhema word from God when I read in Proverbs 24:27 *"Finish your outdoor work and get your fields ready; after that, build your home."* God revealed to me that I was making a mistake by not completing my graduate studies and impressed on me to delay any marriage plans.

I told Ted that the Lord had spoken to me when I had read Proverbs 24 that day and I asked him to read the chapter as well. I didn't tell him what the Lord was speaking to me about. Thankfully, the Lord revealed the same thing to Ted and he picked up the same message when coming to the verse near the end of the chapter. So, we decided to postpone wedding plans, and then I got busy making plans to get back to school.

The Lord confirmed my decision to follow His leading to go back to school in several amazing ways. First, I had an apartment in Houston that I had sub-leased over the summer while I was in Minnesota. I had to start by moving out of that apartment and get an apartment in College Station, Texas. I got an apartment in College Station and a roommate in a few days, by posting my needs on a campus bulletin board.

Then, despite the fact that I had turned down a scholarship that I had received from Landmark Graphics, when I didn't think I was going back to school, I still received the scholarship. I called them up and told them I had changed my mind, and asked if the scholarship was still available. They had not given it to anyone else and said it was still mine if I wanted it.

Next, when I was moving out of my apartment in Houston, I got a phone call from Exxon with an offer of a 3D seismic survey and well data for my Masters Thesis research. I had written them about 9 months earlier asking for this data in order to use it for research. My phone service was still on in the apartment. In those days, people didn't have cellular phones. So, if Exxon had not called that day, I would have missed their call. In fact, I had been gone all summer and that was the ONLY day they could have reached me by phone. What a glorious confirmation! The 3D dataset along with well data was valued at well over $1 million.

Then when I got settled in at Texas A&M, got my classes, and met with my Advisor, I found out that the Geophysics Department at Texas A&M was offering me a Teaching Assistantship in Physical Geology Lab. This Teaching Assistantship normally went to Geology graduate students, but they were going to try a new thing and have a geophysics graduate student teach physical geology lab to the Freshman/Sophomore geophysics students. So, I got the money I needed to complete my graduate degree after having spent the summer in Minnesota as a missionary earning no money. God provided and He miraculously confirmed the decision He spoke to me by reading His Word daily and listening to His prompting *"Finish your outdoor work first and then build your home."*

As an aside note, I did get my MS in Geophysics from Texas A&M in 1988. I worked for Exxon for five years and then I worked for Schlumberger for 24 years. In my career as a geophysicist I got to travel all over the United States, Canada, UK, France, Germany, Austria, The Netherlands, Greece, UAE, Indonesia, Mexico, Brazil, Luanda and many other places. I had a wonderful career with Schlumberger and worked with incredible people from all over the world. I would have missed all of this if I had not followed God's leading me to "finish my outdoor work first". Ted and I did get married in 1989 and have 5 children born between 1994 – 2004. We have been married for 31 years now. God is so good!

Angelic Help

There are three times that I'll share about what I believe was angelic help in my life, although I won't be surprised if I find thousands of instances of angelic help in my life once I get to heaven. The first instance happened when I was driving with two small children in car seats on my way to drop them off to their day care before heading on to work. As I was crossing a major intersection, I ran out of gas. I was able to coast through the intersection, but I had to stop in the left lane of the major street. To my left were the cars that were in line to turn at the left turn signal. As I stopped, I was window-to-window with another car and the woman rolled down her window and I rolled down my window and she asked me if I had run out of gas. I told her I had and that I had two small children in the back seat. I was contemplating what to do. Should I get out on the busy street, get the stroller out from the trunk, get the kids into the stroller and then walk to the nearest gas station? She told me she would get me some gas and come back. What a relief. I took an apple out of my lunch kit and began to eat it. Before I had finished eating the apple, the woman returned and was pouring gas into my car. I had not even taken off my seatbelt. I thanked her and wanted to give her money for buying the gas and helping me out, but she wouldn't take any money. How did she return so quickly? Even if she had a gas can in her car and went to the nearest gas station to fill it and return to me, how did she get back so quickly? I believe she was an angel. The Bible reveals that angels can appear in human form. Hebrews 13:2 says: *"Do not forget to entertain strangers, for by so doing some people have entertained angels without knowing it."*

Another time I was driving about 50 mph on a freeway feeder road with a solid green light in front of me. Moments before crossing the intersection another car completely ran a red light traveling at a high rate of speed. What I realized was that I had removed my foot from the gas pedal moments before. Actually, as I was thinking about it more, my foot was moved for me. I didn't make the conscious decision to let off the gas. In fact, consciously I was wanting to get through the intersection before the light turned yellow. Normally I would keep my foot on the gas to make it through the intersection before the light changed. (I know now this is terrible defensive driving.) But, somehow my foot let off the gas. If I had not done that, I could have easily been hit by the fast-moving vehicle who ran the red light. I believe an angel, invisible this time, prevented the accident by lifting my foot off the gas pedal.

Another time I was driving on a cold and icy Sunday morning on my way to church. I had several kids with me in the van and I was picking up another woman and her children in her apartment complex. As I was driving to her apartment, I hit a patch of ice and it looked like I was going to head straight into the ditch. But then we made it across the ditch….what???? How did that happen? Something like an invisible bridge helped us across the ditch. Certainly, angelic help once again. No accident, no dealing with getting kids out of the car from a ditch on the freezing morning. Just on our way without delay, two mothers with their children on the way to church. Thank you Lord!

The Bible speaks of angelic help. Psalm 91 gives an awesome promise:

> *If you make the Most High your dwelling—even the LORD, who is my refuge—then no harm will befall you, no disaster will come near your tent. For he will command his angels concerning you to guard you in all your ways; they will lift you up in their hands, so that you will not strike your foot against a stone.*
>
> *– Psalm 91:9-12*

Supernatural Miracles

I will share one amazing supernatural miracle that I experienced along with my oldest son, Stefan when he was about 10 years old. We were walking through our neighborhood one night after dinner as the sun was setting. We had walked together several times before and it was a really good time to talk. On this particular evening, Stefan noticed a man ahead of us on our walk through the neighborhood and he was on the curb, looking like he was doing something with the garbage can. Stefan said he didn't feel good about that man and said we should cross to the other side of the street instead of walking by him. We did that and just kept walking and talking. Before long Stefan asked, "Where are we?" I also realized I didn't recognize where we were. Things looked different than our usual walk. We kept walking and then I recognized where we were in the subdivision. Only thing is that it was impossible for us to have gotten there by walking. The streets didn't lead to that street. We were able to walk home fine, but I later drove all over to figure out how we could have ended up where we were. It was impossible. I realized that God had translated us to a different part of the subdivision, maybe to avoid harm from the man Stefan did not feel good about.

The Bible gives an example of such a translation in Acts 8:26-40. Philip had run across an Ethiopian eunuch and was sharing the good news of Jesus Christ with him. The eunuch received the good news of Jesus, understood the passage he was reading in Isaiah 53 was fulfilled in Jesus and he stopped the chariot to be baptized as a new believer in Christ. Then as recorded in the Book of Acts:

> When they came up out of the water, **the Spirit of the Lord suddenly took Philip away**, and the eunuch did not see him again, but went on his way rejoicing. **Philip, however, appeared at Azotus** and traveled about, preaching the gospel in all the towns until he reached Caesarea.
>
> *– Acts 8:39-40*

Overcoming Demonic Attack

A couple of years ago I vividly remember an incident that I'm certain was a demonic attack on me and my youngest daughter. I was home alone and my daughter was at school. I had a super Spirit-filled, pumped-up "Quiet Time" with the Lord that morning and was getting ready for a

Bible study that I was leading at a friend's house. I was sitting in my usual "quiet time chair" finishing my morning reflections when suddenly I got this piercing pain shoot through my head. I'm not one to struggle with headaches or migraines; thankfully it is a very rare event for me to have any kind of ache in my head. But this was such a shock. My hands went up to my head and my eyes closed; it was intense pain, and so sudden. I thought seconds after the pain began that this was a demonic attack, and I spoke out firmly and loudly: "Pain in my head, leave my body NOW in the name of Jesus!" The pain left as quickly as it came. I maybe had to endure the pain for 10 seconds.

That was a weird experience, but I got up and then got ready quickly to head out to my friend's house for the Bible study. As I was driving in my car, my husband called me on my cell phone. He let me know that Christine's school had been trying to reach me because Christine got suddenly sick. I was right by the school as he was talking to me and I pulled over into the parking lot to see what was going on. When I arrived, I was sent to the nurse's office. I know the nurse personally, because we have worshipped together at the same congregation, and when I arrived, Christine was the only one in the nurse's office. The nurse told me she tried to call me, but the phone service never connected. Christine had thrown up so violently that the nurse had to give her new clothes to wear. She was laying down on the bed in the nurse's office and told me her head hurt. When I had dropped her off at school earlier, she was completely fine, not a bit sick or even feeling badly. I told the nurse that I believed it was a demonic attack. We prayed for Christine together for healing and removal of the effects of any demonic attack. I took her home and explained what had happened to me that morning, and that I thought she was going to be just fine. I laid her down on the couch and let her know that I was going ahead to the Bible study I was leading, but to call me if she had any recurrence of the nausea or any trouble. I told her I believed that she would go to sleep and wake up feeling perfectly normal. I went on to the Bible Study and came back a couple of hours later. Christine woke up when I arrived and was totally fine.

The New Testament is filled with occasions when either Jesus or his disciples drove a demon out of someone. The Bible also teaches us that *"our struggle is not against flesh and blood, but against the rulers, against the authorities, against the powers of this dark world and against the spiritual forces of evil in the heavenly realms."* (Ephesians 6:12) Born-again, Spirit-filled believers in Jesus Christ, have authority over demonic forces to command them to leave in the name of Jesus Christ.

Peace in Difficult Trials

Life has its ups and downs for everyone. We all have various kinds of trials and suffering, hardships and difficult circumstances. Without going into explicit detail of what brought me to some extreme lows in my life, I would like to testify of experiences of deep, unexplainable peace in very difficult circumstances. Once, at a time before I was married, the shock of hearing that my parents decided to divorce brought me to such a level of mental anguish that it left me sobbing alone in their bedroom. I was home alone and ended up falling to my knees in my parent's bedroom with my head on their bed. I was way too distraught to even think about praying, and I wasn't spiritually mature enough to think to cry out to God for help. Yet the Lord took over and met me in my time of great need right there in my parent's bedroom. I was transformed from wailing hopelessness to calm assurance. The peace I felt was so amazing that I actually got up from their bedroom and cleaned up the dining room and kitchen from the dinner meal with dancing and singing from the dining room to the kitchen. After God's comforting touch, I had no idea what the future held, but I knew God was going to be there, and He turned my grief into joy. The circumstance did not change, but my attitude of acceptance and peace over it completely changed. The Lord healed my broken heart, strengthened my faith, and filled me with His peace. I later discovered a passage in Psalms 30:11 *"You turned my wailing into dancing."* Although I didn't know it at the time, the Bible says:

Do not be anxious about anything, but in everything, by prayer
and petition, with thanksgiving, present your requests to God.
And the peace of God, which transcends all understanding, will
guard your hearts and your minds in Christ Jesus.

– Philippians 4:6-7

My faith was much more strongly tested during a period of about five years when I was in a trial that could be a book within itself. The drama involved intense pressure, and a strong demonic effort to destroy my husband, our marriage, myself, and at the time, our three children. I can not state strongly enough God sustained me through that time through His Word, His Spirit, my church, and three specific women who held me up in prayer throughout the ordeal. During that time period I continued to work at Schlumberger and at the beginning of the 5-year trial I had received two promotions and three raises in an 11-month period. That increase in salary held our family together financially for the next five years. But what held my mind together was undoubtedly the counsel I received from my Wonderful Counselor through the Holy Bible. I read the Bible every free moment and at the expense of much sleep. The Lord guided me through an extremely tumultuous time period. At one point I was nearly ready to give up. I had endured so much and there was no end in sight. At one low point I did not see how I could keep my family together. I had no transportation, my purse had been stolen, and I had no credit cards, no check book, no money. I had received death threats on my life and my kid's lives. We had to move from our home to another location. It was looking like my husband and I might be permanently separated. I have it dated in my Bible (December 9, 1999) when once again the peace of God completely trumped my circumstances when I received a rhema word from the Lord in the book of Hebrews:

Remember those earlier days after you had received the light,
when you stood your ground in a great contest in the face of
suffering. Sometimes you were publicly exposed to insult and
persecution; at other times you stood side by side with those

who were so treated. You sympathized with those in prison and joyfully accepted the confiscation of your property, because you knew that you yourselves had better and lasting possessions. So do not throw away your confidence; it will be richly rewarded. You need to persevere so that when you have done the will of God, you will receive what He has promised.

— Hebrews 10:32-36

I was at a very low point at that time, but I remember the peace of God that overflowed my life after I read those scriptures and was reminded that God didn't need money, credit cards, or anything to take care of me and my children and to work out our circumstances for good. As it is written in Romans 8:28 *"And we know that in all things God works for the good of those who love him, who have been called according to his purpose".* I didn't need to worry about the future, just make it through each day. And God did bring us through to the other side of that difficult time. Our fourth child was born in January 2002, and we named her Victoria because of the victory that we had achieved in our family by overcoming the five-year trial that had begun in the Summer of 1996.

I've chosen a few events from my life to share in this book to give testimony that God is real, that the Bible has significant, personal impact in my life. Reading God's Word each morning is like having a personal Counseling session with the Creator of the Universe. It is remarkable, and I hope to help many people all over the world realize the truth that the Bible is the most sacred treasure on earth. It is a life-giving book from God.

CHAPTER 15

Conclusion

The Bible is a remarkable book. It is not only a book about God, but from God. I have proven through formulas and numerical patterns that fit together like pieces of a puzzle that key creation scriptures in both the Old and New Testaments have intentional, intelligent mathematical design. I have shown how the gematria of these verses connect to the DNA of all living things by assigning numbers to the 20 common amino acids in DNA through the proton and neutron counts of each amino acid molecule. I challenge anyone to carefully study chapters 1-9, which give the mathematical and scientific evidence of this intelligent design and find any errors I may have made. I did not make any of this up. I discovered these patterns through research, findings in various places on the Internet and personal discovery. It is not interpretation of facts, it is actual facts. After studying these facts, there is only one conclusion, the Bible is from God.

I've also shown how Bible prophecy proves that the Bible is from God as well. The prophecies recorded in Daniel show approximately 600 years of future kingdoms that would come from about 600 BC until near the time of Christ. These prophecies can all be examined through the historical record from other sources outside the Bible. I also briefly showed the major prophecies concerning the coming of Jesus Christ, the promised Messiah, as Savior, paying the penalty for our sins, His first coming as the Suffering Servant. Then I showed 10 of 64 different prophecies in the Bible that declare the Lord would bring the Jews back to their land, Israel, after they had scattered all over the world. Israel became a nation in 1948, remarkably after not being a nation for several thousand years. The study of these prophecies alone is enough to prove the divine nature of the Bible.

I also gave evidence of a few modern-day miracles, that have been documented and references to thousands of other modern-day recorded miracles to show that the miraculous does exist. There is no need to discount the Bible as fiction because of the miracles recorded in it. On the contrary, it gives us more reason for hope and understanding that we are created and our Creator loves us. I also shared a little about my life and how the Lord has worked in my life personally. Personal testimony is evidence.

The Lord gave us a written account of Himself so that we can know Him. This written account, the Bible, is the most sacred treasure that we have on earth. It shows us the Way, the Truth, and the Life (John 14:6), the true way to eternal life and abundant life on earth.

If you consider yourself an atheist or agnostic or simply just don't ever think about God, but you read this book, and realize now that God is real, I invite you to make the decision to invite the Lord Jesus into your life as both Savior and Lord. That means you believe in Jesus, that He died for your sins, and you ask Him to save you and come into your life. He will come into your life and you will be set free from your sins, forgiven, and born spiritually into God's kingdom.

If you are Jewish and believe the Torah and the Tanakh, but don't believe the New Testament is from God, then I urge you to carefully consider the amazing mathematical connection between Genesis 1:1 and John 1:1 as well as all the evidence in Chapters 1-9 that prove the divine inspiration of both the Old and New Testaments, mathematically. You don't have to stop being Jewish to receive Jesus (Yeshua) as the Messiah (Mashiach). You don't stop being Jewish to convert to Christianity. You receive Jesus into your life and become a Messianic Jew, a Jew who believes that Jesus is the Messiah. Most of the first converts were Jewish. The scriptures that the Messiah has not yet fulfilled will be fulfilled at His Second Coming.

If you are Muslim and have learned about God from the Koran, but have been taught that the Bible is not from God, I urge you to read the Bible and ask God to reveal to you the Truth. This book gives solid evidence that the Bible is from God. Jesus died and was resurrected, for the purpose of dying for your sins, my sins and the sins of the whole world so that the penalty of sin would be paid for by Jesus. In order to receive forgiveness for your sins, you must choose to receive Jesus into your life.

If you are Hindu, Buddhist, or any other religious belief, I hope this book will help you understand that the Bible is from God, the one true God, Creator of the Universe, and Creator of you. The Bible is the primary way God speaks to us. It gives us the information we need to choose to receive the Lord Jesus into our lives and live forever with Him and everyone else who is part of His Kingdom. I hope to meet you in Heaven in the future!

ACKNOWLEDGEMENTS

I first of all want to acknowledge and thank my special friend Donna Bell for introducing me to Hebrew. I had no idea how easy the Hebrew alphabet is to learn and how much more in-depth study of the Old Testament is possible knowing even a little bit about Hebrew. I also learned so much about Hebrew from attending Beth Messiah Messianic Jewish Congregation in Houston Texas where about half of the service is conducted in Hebrew, with English subtitle translation. I so enjoyed attending those services with Donna and Steve Bell for over a year. Learning Hebrew from Donna, and the workbook she recommended, *Zola's Introduction to Hebrew* by John Parsons gave me the foundation for the subsequent mathematical discoveries presented in this book. I also appreciate Donna's time editing one of the first pre-published copies I completed.

I also want to acknowledge and thank my friends, Lisa Clark, Connie Sharp, Truly Heiskell, Nina Hoeny and Justin Oneacre for their prayers, support, reviews, edits, and suggestions. I love you dear friends and I'm so grateful for you.

I highly acknowledge the work of John Nuyten and his two websites, LivingGreekNT.org and the livingword.org.au. As I was getting into this study, I asked the Lord if He could just translate me to Heaven temporarily, kind of like He did to Josiah (see Miracle section), so I could learn from Him directly about all the mathematical design in the scriptures. Instead, He pointed me to John Nuyten's websites! Likewise, Peter Bluer's YouTube videos on Bible Numerics are awesome. The "Bible Wheel" work of R.A. McGough, which he later debunked, was also very valuable to me. I'm beyond grateful he left his wonderful database posted on the Internet that helped me look up numbers that correlate to words and verses in the Bible. Much of the things I discovered in this book, I would not have been able to find without access to his database.

I also want to thank my wonderful husband for enabling me to write this book. When I took a surprise "early retirement" from Schlumberger, we were not exactly ready, financially, for me to retire. I'm grateful for his support of me and our family, with four of our five children in college. Thank you for your support for me to work on this "assignment from the Lord".

Lastly, and mostly, I thank you, Lord Jesus, for saving me and taking me on this journey of revelation. So many times, I was absolutely jaw-opened, speechless, amazed beyond measure, praising You with all my heart, as You led me through discovering all these mathematical and DNA-connecting puzzle pieces. It was so much fun to call Connie practically every other day to tell her what next You had revealed to me. I know You as my Wonderful Counselor, and I know You in a special way in Proverbs 25:2 "*It is the glory of God to conceal a matter; to search out a matter is the glory of kings.*" I am so grateful to be a Princess in Your Kingdom.

APPENDIX 1

Original Languages of Scripture

Old Testament

The books of the Old Testament, referred to by the Jews as the *Tanakh*, were predominantly written in Hebrew. Some minor portions, 268 verses of the Old Testament, were originally written in Aramaic. The portions of Scripture that were written in Aramaic include Ezra 4:8-6:18 and 7:12-26 (67 verses), Daniel 2:4b-7:28 (200 verses), Jeremiah 10:11, and various proper names and single words and phrases scattered throughout the Old and New Testaments.[1] Aramaic was introduced to the Hebrews as the spoken language when the Israelites were taken to Babylon during the 70 years of Babylonian captivity. That is why Daniel, who was one of the captives taken to Babylon, writes in both Hebrew and Aramaic in the Book of Daniel.

The Old Testament writings have been preserved in Hebrew to the present day. The preservation of the Hebrew scriptures is significant. Jewish scribes have meticulously preserved the Hebrew scriptures from the original writings in the original Hebrew. For example, the first five books of the Old Testament are referred to by the Jews as the *Torah* and contain exactly 304,804 well-formed Hebrew letters in 248 columns.[2] Also, any enlargement of certain letters has been preserved as well. So, when scholars study the Torah or other Old Testament scriptures, it is from the original language, Hebrew.

Scripture readings from the Torah and other parts of the Tanach in Jewish services have been and continue to be read in Hebrew. I have attended a Messianic Jewish Congregation in Houston, Texas, and have listened to the reading of the scripture in Hebrew with English translation posted on the screen. It is interesting to note that this practice of reading the scriptures in Hebrew with common language translation has been practiced in Jewish synagogues for centuries, and definitely in the time of Christ.

In the article, "Jewish Languages: From Aramaic to Yiddish", it states: "During the Talmudic era, Hebrew illiteracy was so high that the Shabbat Torah reading was recited along with a verse-by-verse translation into Aramaic."[3] Thus, the reading of the Torah in Jewish services on the Sabbath, the seventh day of the week, has continued throughout the centuries to be read in Hebrew while translated into the common language.

New Testament

The New Testament is commonly believed to have been originally written in Greek, although the language most probably spoken by Jesus to his disciples and among the Jews was Aramaic. There is some debate over whether the original language of the New Testament Scriptures is Greek or Aramaic. It is not absolutely certain, if the original writing of the New Testament, or at least some of the books were originally written in Aramaic and then shortly thereafter translated into Greek, or vice versa.

Dr. Thomas S. McCall, Th.M. in Old Testament Studies and Th.D. in Semitic languages and Old Testament, who writes in his article "The Language of the Gospel":

"It seems fairly certain that the Gospels of Luke and John, the Book of Acts, the Epistles, and the Book of Revelation were originally written in Greek." He also states "The oldest known manuscripts of Matthew and Mark are in Greek. According to recent scholarship, Greek fragments of these two Gospels have been verified as dating from as early as the 60s A.D. Some scholars have argued that these Gospels were originally written in Aramaic and later translated into Greek. If that is the case, no extant copies or fragments of the Aramaic text have been found. The only evidence we have is that the original text of Matthew and Mark was in Greek."[4]

Although Aramaic was a common language for the Jews living in Judea and Galilee around the time of Christ, Greek was also a common Gentile language of the day. Some, if not many, Jews probably were bilingual or trilingual knowing both Aramaic and Greek, as well as Hebrew. And some may have been quadrilingual knowing Latin as well. When Jesus was crucified the sign Pilate placed above Jesus said "Jesus of Nazareth, the King of the Jews" and it was written in Aramaic, Latin and Greek (John 19:19-20). It is also interesting to note that in Matthew 27:46, it is recorded that Jesus cried out from the cross "Eloi, Eloi, lama sabachthani?", which is a mixture of Aramaic and Hebrew, and is then translated in the verse "which means, 'My God, my God, why have you forsaken me?'" If Matthew wrote his Gospel in Aramaic, why would he translate what this portion of Jesus' statement meant? It seems more logical that Matthew wrote in the common language of the day, Greek, to get the message out to the "farthest part of the world".

Likewise, in Mark 5 Jesus raises Jairus's daughter, the daughter of the synagogue ruler, from the dead. The miracle is recorded with Jesus' statement in a mixture of Aramaic and Hebrew, while the rest of the verse is in the common Greek language.

> He took her by the hand and said to her, **"Talitha Koum!"**
> (which means, "Little girl, I say to you, get up!").
>
> – Mark 5:41

This is another example that if the original text was written in Aramaic, the author would not explain the meaning of the phrase that Jesus stated in Aramaic. Talitha in Aramaic means "little girl". There is no Hebrew equivalent that sound like "Talitha". However, "koum" is the same Hebrew word in Isaiah 60:1 (*Arise, shine, for your light has come, and the glory of the LORD has risen on you!*) pronounced "koumy" which means arise.

In any case, the verses that we will look at in Greek, show mathematical phenomena similar to the phenomena of the Hebrew scriptures. So, I believe it is fairly safe to assume that the mathematical phenomena found in the New Testament scriptures, in Greek, is part of the intelligent mathematical design of the written Word of God. I did some study of the scriptures in Aramaic, but I did not find any mathematical phenomena using this language.

APPENDIX 2

Words in the Bible with a Gematria of 37

	Hebrew	Hebrew / English	First Occurrence
1	ויהיו	hayah / was	Genesis 2:25
2	ולא	lo / not	Genesis 2:25
3	ואל	el / unto	Genesis 3:16
4	הבל	Hebel / Abel	Genesis 4:2
5	כטוב	towb / good	Genesis 19:8
6	ואיך	eyk / how	Genesis 26:9
7	גדל	gadal / magnify	Genesis 26:13
8	לוא	lo / not	Genesis 31:35
9	וייטב	yatab / well	Genesis 41:37
10	והכבד	kabad / honor	Exodus 8:15
11	ויחזו	chazah / see	Exodus 24:11
12	לגד	Gad / Gad	Numbers 1:14
13	דגל	degel / standard	Numbers 2:3
14	יחידה	yachiyd / only	Judges 11:34
15	לבה	leb / heart	Judges 19:3
16	יכבה	kabah / quenched	1 Samuel 3:3
17	אלו	el / unto	1 Samuel 22:13
18	אחזיהו	Achazyah / Ahaziah	1 Kings 22:40
19	ואחזיה	Achazyah / Ahaziah	2 Kings 9:16
20	יהואחז	Yehowachaz / Jehoahaz	2 Kings 10:35
21	אכביד	kabad / honor	2 Chronicles 10:14
22	זכי	Zakkay / Zaccai	Ezra 2:9
23	חטיטא	Chatiyta / Hatita	Ezra 2:42
24	אלהא	elahh (Aramaic) / God	Ezra 4:24

Appendix 2 Continued

	Hebrew	Hebrew / English	First Occurrence
25	לֹאבַד	abad / perish	Esther 8:5
26	לֶהַב	lahab / flame	Job 39:23
27	יביטו	nabat / look	Job 39:29
28	הכבוד	kabowd / glory	Psalm 24:7
29	טוּבְךָ	tuwb / goodness	Psalm 25:7
30	ואודך	yadah / praise	Psalm 43:4
31	כבודה	kebuwddah / carriage	Psalm 45:13
32	יהבך	yehab / burden	Psalm 55:22
33	ויזובו	zuwb / flow	Psalm 78:20
34	הכזה	zeh / this	Isaiah 58:5
35	הלב	leb / heart	Jeremiah 17:9
36	הדיחי	nadach / drive	Jeremiah 27:15
37	וכאחב	Achab / Ahab	Jeremiah 29:22
38	ביהודי	Yehuwdiy / Jew	Jeremiah 34:9
39	והכו	nakah / smite	Jeremiah 37:15
40	והביטה	nabat / look	Lamentations 1:11
41	בלה	balah / wax	Lamentations 3:4
42	וחזוי	chezev (Aramaic) / vision	Daniel 2:28
43	כחדה	chad (Aramaic) / one	Daniel 2:35
44	לדג	dag / fish	Jonah 2:10
45	כדגי	dag / fish	Habakkuk 1:14
46	היחיד	yachiyd / only	Zechariah 12:10
47	ηιδει	eido / know	Matthew 24:43
48	εθεαθη	theaomai / see	Mark 16:11
49	αγιαζει	hagiazo / sanctify	Hebrews 9:13

Historical Archive of the Bible Wheel Site, Full Text Hebrew/ Greek Bible Gematria Database, https://www.biblewheel.com/GR/ GR Database.php?Gem Number=37&SearchByNum=Go

APPENDIX 3

HOW I DERIVED THE STATISTICAL ANALYSIS OF GENESIS 1:1, JOHN 1:1 AND PROVERBS 30:6 CONNECTING DIRECTLY WITH THE NUCLEON MATRIX.

First, I will show how I derived that there are 65,535 unique number combinations that can be added in the Nucleon Matrix of 16 numbers. The formula to determine the number of combinations possible for any given number of items is

$$\frac{n!}{r!(n-r)!}$$

Where n = total number of items, r = number of items from the total that will be combined. For a matrix of 16 numbers, if I only want to pull one number from the total, there are 16 unique one-number combinations. If I want to pull two numbers from the total of 16 numbers, then there are 120 possible combinations as the formula below shows.

$$\frac{16!}{2!(16-2)!} = \frac{16 \times 15}{2} = 120$$

I won't list all 120 combinations here, but to get the idea, if I take the "items" A, B, C, D, E, F, G, H, I, J, K, L, M, N, O, P (16 letters) the combinations are AB, AC, AD, AE, AF, AG, AH, AI, AJ, AK, AL, AM, AN, AO, AP 15 combinations of two numbers that begin with A, 14 combinations of two numbers that begin with B, 13 combinations of two numbers that begin with C, 12 combinations of numbers that begin with D, 11 combinations of numbers that begin with E and so on. Since with the Nucleon Matrix, the items are numbers, not letters, I only use AB and not BA, because A+B = B+A.

However, you can also combine any three numbers or any four numbers, any five numbers, all the way up to any 15 numbers. Then there is only one combination of all 16 numbers. The table below shows all the possible combinations totaling to 65,535.

Possible permutations with 1 number	16
Possible permutations with 2 numbers	120
Possible permutations with 3 numbers	560
Possible permutations with 4 numbers	1820
Possible permutations with 5 numbers	4368
Possible permutations with 6 numbers	8008
Possible permutations with 7 numbers	11440
Possible permutations with 8 numbers	12870
Possible permutations with 9 numbers	11440
Possible permutations with 10 numbers	8008
Possible permutations with 11 numbers	4368
Possible permutations with 12 numbers	1820
Possible permutations with 13 numbers	560
Possible permutations with 14 numbers	120
Possible permutations with 15 numbers	16
Possible permutations with 16 numbers	1
Total number of permutations possible using 16 numbers	65535

Next, to determine the random selection of three verses in the Bible, since there are 30,054 verses in the Bible, there are 4.52389×10^{12} possibilities of randomly selecting 3 verses out of the Bible as shown in the formula below.

$$\frac{30054!}{3!(30054-3)!} = \frac{30054!}{6(30051!)} = \frac{30054 \times 30053 \times 30052}{6} = 4.52389 \times 10^{12}$$

For these three random verses to connect precisely with the Nucleon Matrix, I multiplied the two statistics together, $65{,}535 \times 4.52389 \times 10^{12} = 2.96473 \times 10^{17}$

To be honest, I'm not certain that the way I did this statistical analysis is totally accurate, however, I hope you see the point that it is highly unlikely that this is a random connection rather than a purposeful design.

APPENDIX 4

Numbers from Neutron Matrix that add to 2300, connecting with Genesis 1:1

#	320	282	272	264	258	256	246	236	220	212	212	210	196	170	164	140	=	2300
1	320	282	272	264	258		246	236		212		210					=	2300
2	320	282	272	264	258				220			210		170	164	140	=	2300
3	320	282	272	264		256	246	236		212	212						=	2300
4	320	282	272	264		256		236					196	170	164	140	=	2300
5	320	282	272	264		256			220	212				170	164	140	=	2300
6	320	282	272		258	256	246	236	220			210					=	2300
7	320	282	272		258		246	236		212				170	164	140	=	2300
8	320	282	272		258			236	220	212			196		164	140	=	2300
9	320	282	272			256	246			212	212		196		164	140	=	2300
10	320	282	272					236	220	212	212	210	196			140	=	2300
11	320	282		264	258		246		220			210	196		164	140	=	2300
12	320	282		264	258		246			212	212		196	170		140	=	2300
13	320	282		264			246	236	220	212		210		170		140	=	2300
14	320	282		264			246	236		212		210	196	170	164		=	2300
15	320	282		264			246		220	212	212	210		170	164		=	2300
16	320	282				256	246	236	220			210	196	170	164		=	2300
17	320		272	264	258	256	246					210		170	164	140	=	2300
18	320		272	264	258	256		236	220					170	164	140	=	2300
19	320		272	264	258	256			220			210	196		164	140	=	2300
20	320		272	264	258	256				212	212		196	170		140	=	2300
21	320		272	264		256		236	220	212		210		170		140	=	2300
22	320		272	264		256			220	212	212	210		170	164		=	2300
23	320		272		258	256	246	236		212			196		164	140	=	2300
24	320		272		258		246	236		212	212	210		170	164		=	2300
25	320		272		258			236	220	212	212	210	196		164		=	2300
26	320		272			256	246	236		212	212	210	196			140	=	2300
27	320			264	258		246	236	220	212		210		170	164		=	2300
28	320			264		256	246	236	220	212	212			170	164		=	2300
29	320			264		256	246	236	220	212		210	196			140	=	2300
30	320			264		256	246		220	212	212	210	196		164		=	2300
31	320				258	256	246		220	212	212	210	196	170			=	2300
32		282	272	264	258	256				212	212	210		170	164		=	2300
33		282	272	264	258		246	236	220	212				170		140	=	2300
34		282	272	264	258		246	236		212			196	170	164		=	2300
35		282	272	264	258		246		220	212	212			170	164		=	2300
36		282	272	264	258		246		220	212		210	196			140	=	2300
37		282	272	264	258	256		236		212		210		170		140	=	2300
38		282	272	264	258		246		220	212	212			170	164		=	2300
39		282	272	264		256	246		220	212	212		196			140	=	2300
40		282	272	264			246	236		212	212	210	196	170			=	2300
41		282	272		258	256	246	236	220				196	170	164		=	2300
42		282	272			256	246	236	220	212		210	196	170			=	2300
43		282		264	258	256	246	236		212	212			170	164		=	2300
44		282		264	258	256	246	236		212		210	196			140	=	2300
45		282		264	258	256	246		220	212	212	210				140	=	2300
46		282		264	258	256	246			212	212	210	196		164		=	2300
47		282		264	258	256		236	220	212	212		196		164		=	2300
48			272	264	258	256	246	236	220	212			196			140	=	2300
49			272	264	258	256	246		220	212	212		196		164		=	2300
50			272	264	258		246	236	220	212	212	210		170			=	2300

Numbers from the Neutron Matrix that add to 1492, Connecting with Genesis 1:1

#	320	282	272	264	258	256	246	236	220	212	212	210	196	170	164	140	=	1492
1	320	282	272		258				220							140	=	1492
2	320	282	272		258								196		164		=	1492
3	320	282	272					236		212				170			=	1492
4	320	282	272							212		210	196				=	1492
5	320	282		264			246					210		170			=	1492
6	320	282		264				236	220					170			=	1492
7	320	282		264					220			210	196				=	1492
8	320	282			258	256		236								140	=	1492
9	320	282			258	256				212					164		=	1492
10	320	282				256				212	212	210					=	1492
11	320	282					246	236		212			196				=	1492
12	320	282					246		220	212	212						=	1492
13	320	282							220				196	170	164	140	=	1492
14	320		272	264		256						210		170			=	1492
15	320		272	264			246		220					170			=	1492
16	320		272		258	256	246									140	=	1492
17	320		272		258			236				210	196				=	1492
18	320		272		258				220	212		210					=	1492
19	320		272			256		236		212			196				=	1492
20	320		272			256			220	212	212						=	1492
21	320			264		256	246	236						170			=	1492
22	320			264		256	246					210	196				=	1492
23	320			264		256		236	220				196				=	1492
24	320				258	256		236		212		210					=	1492
25	320				258		246	236	220	212							=	1492
26	320					256	246						196	170	164	140	=	1492
27	320							236	220			210	196	170		140	=	1492
28	320								220	212		210	196	170	164		=	1492
29		282	272	264	258		246							170			=	1492
30		282	272	264	258				220				196				=	1492
31		282	272		258	256				212	212						=	1492
32		282	272						220	212			196	170		140	=	1492
33		282	272							212	212	210			164	140	=	1492
34		282		264	258	256		236					196				=	1492
35		282		264	258	256			220	212							=	1492
36		282		264				236				210	196		164	140	=	1492
37		282		264						220	212	210			164	140	=	1492
38		282			258			236				210	196	170		140	=	1492
39		282			258				220	212		210		170		140	=	1492
40		282			258					212		210	196	170	164		=	1492
41		282				256		236		212			196	170		140	=	1492
42		282				256			220	212	212			170		140	=	1492
43		282				256				212	212		196	170	164		=	1492
44		282					246	236		212	212				164	140	=	1492
45			272	264	258	256	246						196				=	1492
46			272	264			246	236						170	164	140	=	1492
47			272	264			246					210	196		164	140	=	1492
48			272	264				236	220				196		164	140	=	1492
49			272		258		246					210	196	170		140	=	1492
50			272		258			236	220				196	170		140	=	1492
51			272		258			236		212		210			164	140	=	1492
52			272		258				220	212			196	170	164		=	1492
53			272			256	246			212			196	170		140	=	1492
54			272			256		236		212	212				164	140	=	1492
55				264	258			236	220			210			164	140	=	1492
56				264	258			236		212	212			170		140	=	1492
57				264	258					212	212	210	196			140	=	1492
58				264		256	246		220				196	170		140	=	1492
59				264		256	246			212		210			164	140	=	1492
60				264		256		236	220	212					164	140	=	1492
61					258	256	246			212		210		170		140	=	1492
62					258	256		236	220	212				170		140	=	1492
63					258	256		236		212			196	170	164		=	1492
64					258	256			220	212	212			170	164		=	1492
65					258	256			220	212		210	196			140	=	1492

APPENDIX 5

Numbers from the Neutron Matrix that add to 1306, connecting with John 1:1

#	320	282	272	264	258	256	246	236	220	212	212	210	196	170	164	140		1306
1	320	282	272					236					196				=	1306
2	320	282	272						220	212							=	1306
3	320	282			258			236				210					=	1306
4	320	282				256		236		212							=	1306
5	320		272		258		246					210					=	1306
6	320		272		258			236	220								=	1306
7	320		272			256	246			212							=	1306
8	320			264		256	246		220								=	1306
9	320				258					212	212				164	140	=	1306
10	320						246		220			210		170		140	=	1306
11	320						246					210	196	170	164		=	1306
12	320							236	220				196	170	164		=	1306
13		282	272				246						196	170		140	=	1306
14		282	272					236		212					164	140	=	1306
15		282		264	258	256	246										=	1306
16		282		264			246					210			164	140	=	1306
17		282		264				236	220						164	140	=	1306
18		282		264						212	212		196			140	=	1306
19		282			258		246					210		170		140	=	1306
22		282			258			236	220					170		140	=	1306
23		282			258			236					196	170	164		=	1306
24		282			256				220	212				170	164		=	1306
25		282			258				220			210	196			140	=	1306
26		282				256	246			212				170		140	=	1306
27		282				256			220	212			196			140	=	1306
28		282						236		212		210	196	170			=	1306
29		282							220	212	212	210		170			=	1306
30			272	264		256						210			164	140	=	1306
31			272	264			246		220						164	140	=	1306
32			272		258	256						210		170		140	=	1306
33			272		258		246		220					170		140	=	1306
34			272		258		246						196	170	164		=	1306
35			272				246			212		210	196	170			=	1306
36			272					236	220	212			196	170			=	1306
37			272					236		212	212	210			164		=	1306
38				264	258			236		212			196			140	=	1306
39				264	258				220	212	212					140	=	1306
40				264	258					212	212		196		164		=	1306
41				264		256	246	236							164	140	=	1306
42				264			246		220			210	196	170			=	1306
43				264				236	220	212		210			164		=	1306
44					258	256	246	236						170		140	=	1306
45					258	256	246			212				170	164		=	1306
46					258	256	246					210	196			140	=	1306
47					258	256		236	220				196			140	=	1306
48					258	256			220	212			196		164		=	1306
49					258			236	220	212		210		170			=	1306
50						256	246			212	212	210		170			=	1306
51						256		236	220	212	212			170			=	1306
52						256			220	212	212	210	196				=	1306

Appendix 5 Continued

Numbers from the Neutron Matrix that add to 1536, Connecting with John 1:1

#	320	282	272	264	258	256	246	236	220	212	212	210	196	170	164	140	= 1536
1	320	282	272	264	258											140	= 1536
2	320	282	272			256		236						170			= 1536
3	320	282	272			256						210	196				= 1536
4	320	282	272				246		220				196				= 1536
5	320	282		264			246			212	212						= 1536
6	320	282		264									196	170	164	140	= 1536
7	320	282			258		246		220			210					= 1536
8	320	282				256	246	236					196				= 1536
9	320	282				256	246		220	212							= 1536
10	320		272	264	258					212		210					= 1536
11	320		272		258					212				170	164	140	= 1536
12	320		272							212	212	210		170		140	= 1536
13	320			264	258		246	236		212							= 1536
14	320			264	258				220					170	164	140	= 1536
15	320			264				236				210	196	170		140	= 1536
16	320			264					220	212		210		170		140	= 1536
17	320			264						212		210	196	170	164		= 1536
18	320				258	256	246	236	220								= 1536
19	320				258		246			212			196		164	140	= 1536
20	320					256			220			210	196	170	164		= 1536
21	320						246	236	220			210			164	140	= 1536
22	320						246	236		212	212			170		140	= 1536
23	320						246			212	212	210	196			140	= 1536
24	320							236	220	212	212		196			140	= 1536
25		282	272	264						212			196	170		140	= 1536
26		282	272			256			220				196	170		140	= 1536
27		282	272			256				212		210			164	140	= 1536
28		282	272				246	236					196		164	140	= 1536
29		282	272				246		220	212					164	140	= 1536
30		282		264	258					212		210		170		140	= 1536
31		282		264		256			220			210			164	140	= 1536
32		282		264		256				212	212			170		140	= 1536
33		282			258	256			220			210		170		140	= 1536
34		282			258		246	236				210			164	140	= 1536
35		282			258			236		212	212		196			140	= 1536
36		282				256	246	236		212					164	140	= 1536
37			272	264	258			236					196	170		140	= 1536
38			272	264	258				220	212				170		140	= 1536
39			272	264	258					212			196	170	164		= 1536
40			272	264				236	220			210		170	164		= 1536
41			272		258	256		236				210			164	140	= 1536
42			272		258	256			220				196	170	164		= 1536
43			272		258		246	236	220						164	140	= 1536
44			272		258		246			212	212		196			140	= 1536
45			272				246	236	220	212		210				140	= 1536
46			272				246	236		212		210	196		164		= 1536
47				264	258	256		236		212				170		140	= 1536
48				264	258	256				212		210	196			140	= 1536
49				264	258		246		220	212			196			140	= 1536

Appendix 5 Continued

Numbers from the Neutron Matrix that add to 816, Connecting with John 1:1

#	272	246	236	220	210	196	170	164	140		
1	272				210		170	164		=	816
2		246	236				170	164		=	816
3		246		220	210				140	=	816
4		246			210	196		164		=	816
5			236	220		196		164		=	816

Neutron Matrix

256	258	246	220
264	140	212	164
170	210	272	196
282	320	236	212

APPENDIX 6

Numbers from the Proton Matrix that Correlate With Genesis 1:1

#																		=	
1	376	320	320	300	300			288				236				160		=	2300
2	376	320	320	300	300				256			236		192				=	2300
3	376	320	320	300				288	256		248			192				=	2300
4	376	320	320	300					256	256	248		224					=	2300
5	376	320	320					288	256	256	248	236						=	2300
6	376	320	320						256		248	236		192	192	160		=	2300
7	376	320		300	300	296					248	236	224					=	2300
8	376	320		300	300			288	256			236	224					=	2300
9	376	320		300	300							236	224	192	192	160		=	2300
10	376	320		300				288			248		224	192	192	160		=	2300
11	376	320		300					256	256	248			192	192	160		=	2300
12	376	320						288	256		248	236	224	192		160		=	2300
13	376	320							256	256	248	236	224	192	192			=	2300
14	376			300	300	296		288	256		248	236						=	2300
15	376			300	300	296					248	236		192	192	160		=	2300
16	376			300	300			288	256			236		192	192	160		=	2300
17	376			300	300				256	256		236	224	192		160		=	2300
18	376			300				288	256	256	248		224	192		160		=	2300
19		320	320	300	300						248	236	224	192		160		=	2300
20		320	320	300		296	296	288	256				224					=	2300
21		320	320	300		296	296						224	192	192	160		=	2300
22		320	320			296	296	288				236		192	192	160		=	2300
23		320	320			296	296		256			236	224	192		160		=	2300
24		320		300	300			288	256		248	236		192		160		=	2300
25		320		300	300			288			248	236	224	192	192			=	2300
26		320		300	300				256	256	248	236	224			160		=	2300
27		320		300	300				256	256	248	236		192	192			=	2300
28		320		300		296	296	288	256					192	192	160		=	2300
29		320		300		296	296		256	256			224	192		160		=	2300
30		320				296	296	288	256	256		236		192		160		=	2300
31		320				296	296	288	256			236	224	192	192			=	2300
32				300	300			288	256	256	248	236	224	192				=	2300
33				300		296	296	288	256	256			224	192	192			=	2300

#																		=	
1	376			300		296	296						224					=	1492
2	376					296	296	288				236						=	1492
3		320	320	300		296			256									=	1492
4		320		300		296							224	192		160		=	1492
5		320				296		288				236		192		160		=	1492
6		320				296			256			236	224			160		=	1492
7		320				296			256			236		192	192			=	1492
8				300		296	296				248			192		160		=	1492
9				300		296		288	256					192		160		=	1492
10				300		296		288					224	192	192			=	1492
11				300		296			256	256			224			160		=	1492
12				300		296			256	256				192	192			=	1492
13						296	296		256		248	236				160		=	1492
14						296	296				248	236	224	192				=	1492
15						296		288	256	256		236				160		=	1492
16						296		288	256			236	224	192				=	1492

Numbers from the Proton Matrix that Correlate With John 1:1

#																	=	
1	376	320				296							224			160	=	1376
2	376	320				296								192	192		=	1376
3	376					296	296				248					160	=	1376
4	376					296		288	256							160	=	1376
5	376					296		288					224	192			=	1376
6	376					296			256	256				192			=	1376
7		320	320			296					248			192			=	1376
8		320	320					288	256					192			=	1376
9		320	320						256	256			224				=	1376
10		320		300	300	296										160	=	1376
11		320		300		296						236	224				=	1376
12		320				296		288			248		224				=	1376
13		320						288					224	192	192	160	=	1376
14		320							256	256				192	192	160	=	1376
15				300	300	296		288						192			=	1376
16				300	300	296			256				224				=	1376
17				300		296		288	256			236					=	1376
18				300		296						236		192	192	160	=	1376
19						296		288			248			192	192	160	=	1376
20						296			256		248		224	192		160	=	1376
21								288	256	256			224	192		160	=	1376

#																	=	
1	376	320	320			296							224				=	1536
2	376	320				296	296				248						=	1536
3	376	320				296		288	256								=	1536
4	376	320				296								192	192	160	=	1536
5	376					296		288					224	192		160	=	1536
6	376					296			256	256				192		160	=	1536
7	376					296			256				224	192	192		=	1536
8		320	320	300	300	296											=	1536
9		320	320			296					248			192		160	=	1536
10		320	320					288	256					192		160	=	1536
11		320	320					288					224	192	192		=	1536
12		320	320						256	256			224			160	=	1536
13		320	320						256	256				192	192		=	1536
14		320		300		296						236	224			160	=	1536
15		320		300		296						236		192	192		=	1536
16		320				296		288			248		224			160	=	1536
17		320				296		288			248			192	192		=	1536
18		320				296			256	256	248					160	=	1536
19		320				296			256		248		224	192			=	1536
20		320				296			256		248		224	192			=	1536
21		320						288	256	256			224	192			=	1536
22				300	300	296		288						192		160	=	1536
23				300	300	296			256				224			160	=	1536
24				300	300	296			256					192	192		=	1536
25				300		296	296				248	236				160	=	1536
26				300		296		288	256			236				160	=	1536
27				300		296		288				236	224	192			=	1536
28				300		296			256	256		236		192			=	1536
29						296		288	256	256	248			192			=	1536

APPENDIX 8

Numbers from the Nucleon, Proton and Neutron Matrices that Correlate with Genesis 1:27

So God created man in His own image
In the image of God He created Him
Male and female He created them.

The gematria of Genesis 1:27 is 2816.

The numbers from the Nucleon Matrix that add to 2816 are:

#																	
1	696	592									446	420	362		300	=	2816
2	696		560			542							362	356	300	=	2816
3	696		560	558		542				460						=	2816
4	696			558						460	446			356	300	=	2816
5	696					542		476			446			356	300	=	2816
6	602	592			556	542	524									=	2816
7	602		560				524		468				362		300	=	2816
8	602		560					476		460			362	356		=	2816
9	602			558			524	476						356	300	=	2816
10	602			558				476		460		420			300	=	2816
11	602				556	542				460				356	300	=	2816
12	602						524	476	468		446				300	=	2816
13	602						524		468		446	420		356		=	2816
14		592	560		556						446		362		300	=	2816
15		592	560			542				460			362		300	=	2816
16		592	560					476	468			420			300	=	2816
17		592		558		542			468					356	300	=	2816
18		592				542		476		460	446				300	=	2816
19		592				542				460	446	420		356		=	2816
20			560	558				476			446	420		356		=	2816
21				558	556		524			460			362	356		=	2816
22					556	542	524	476					362	356		=	2816
23					556	542		476		460		420	362			=	2816
24					556		524		468	460	446		362			=	2816

The numbers from the Proton Matrix that add to 2816 are:

#																		
1	376	320	320	300	300	296	296		256					192		160	=	2816
2	376	320	320	300	300	296	296						224	192	192		=	2816
3	376	320	320	300		296	296	288				236	224			160	=	2816
4	376	320	320	300		296	296	288				236		192	192		=	2816
5	376	320	320	300		296	296		256	256		236				160	=	2816
6	376	320	320	300		296	296		256			236	224	192			=	2816
7	376	320	320			296	296	288	256	256	248					160	=	2816
8	376	320	320			296	296	288	256		248		224	192			=	2816
9	376	320		300	300	296	296	288	256				224			160	=	2816
10	376	320		300	300	296	296	288	256					192	192		=	2816
11	376	320		300	300	296	296		256	256			224	192			=	2816
12	376	320		300		296	296	288	256	256		236		192			=	2816
13	376			300		296	296	288	256			236	224	192	192	160	=	2816
14		320	320	300	300	296	296	288	256		248			192			=	2816
15		320	320	300	300	296	296		256	256	248		224				=	2816
16		320	320	300	300	296			256	256			224	192	192	160	=	2816
17		320	320	300		296	296	288	256	256	248	236					=	2816
18		320	320	300		296	296		256		248	236		192	192	160	=	2816
19		320	320	300		296		288	256	256		236		192	192	160	=	2816
20		320		300	300	296	296	288			248		224	192	192	160	=	2816
21		320		300	300	296	296		256	256	248			192	192	160	=	2816
22		320		300		296	296	288	256		248	236	224	192		160	=	2816
23		320		300		296	296		256	256	248	236	224	192	192		=	2816
24				300	300	296	296	288	256	256	248		224	192		160	=	2816

The numbers from the Neutron Matrix that add to 2816 are:

#																		
1	320	282	272	264	258	256		236		212		210	196	170		140	=	2816
2	320	282	272	264	258	256			220	212	212	210		170		140	=	2816
3	320	282	272	264	258	256				212	212	210	196	170	164		=	2816
4	320	282	272	264	258		246	236	220	212			196	170		140	=	2816
5	320	282	272	264	258		246	236		212	212	210			164	140	=	2816
6	320	282	272	264	258		246		220	212	212		196	170	164		=	2816
7	320	282	272		258	256	246	236	220	212		210			164	140	=	2816
8	320	282		264	258	256	246	236	220	212	212			170		140	=	2816
9	320	282		264	258	256	246	236		212	212		196	170	164		=	2816
10	320	282		264	258	256	246		220	212	212	210	196			140	=	2816
11	320		272	264	258		246	236	220	212	212	210	196	170			=	2816
12		282	272	264	258	256	246	236	220	212		210	196		164		=	2816
13		282	272			256	246	236	220	212	212	210	196	170	164	140	=	2816

Numbers from the Nucleon Matrix that Correlate with Genesis 2:23

This is now bone of my bones and flesh of my flesh.
She shall be called 'woman' for she was taken out of man.

The gematria of these two phrases in Genesis 2:23 is 4000.

The numbers from the Nucleon Matrix that add to 4000 are:

#																		
1	696	602	592	560	558			524		468							=	4000
2	696	602	592	560						468			420	362		300	=	4000
3	696	602	592		558				476				420		356	300	=	4000
4	696	602	592						476	468		446	420			300	=	4000
5	696	602		560	558				476			446		362		300	=	4000
6	696	602		560	558					468	460				356	300	=	4000
7	696	602		560	558							446	420	362	356		=	4000
8	696	602		560			542	524					420		356	300	=	4000
9	696	602		560			542		476	468					356	300	=	4000
10	696		592		558	556			476		460			362		300	=	4000
11	696		592		558	556					460		420	362	356		=	4000
12	696		592			556	542		476				420	362	356		=	4000
13	696		592			556		524		468		446		362	356		=	4000
14	696		592			556				468	460	446	420	362			=	4000
15	696		592				542	524		468	460			362	356		=	4000
16	696			560	558			524	476	468				362	356		=	4000
17	696			560	558				476	468	460		420	362			=	4000
18	696			560		556	542	524			460			362		300	=	4000
19	696			560		556	542			468	460			362	356		=	4000
20	696			560		556		524	476	468			420			300	=	4000
21	696				558	556	542	524		468					356	300	=	4000
22	696				558	556	542			468	460		420			300	=	4000
23	696					556	542	524	476		460	446				300	=	4000
24	696					556	542	524			460	446	420		356		=	4000
25	696					556	542		476	468	460	446			356		=	4000

Continued on next page

Continued from previous page

26	602	592	560	558	556			476						356	300	=	4000
27	602	592	560	558			524				446		362	356		=	4000
28	602	592	560	558						460	446	420	362			=	4000
29	602	592	560		556		524				446	420			300	=	4000
30	602	592	560		556			476	468		446				300	=	4000
31	602	592	560		556				468		446	420		356		=	4000
32	602	592	560			542	524			460		420			300	=	4000
33	602	592	560			542		476	468	460					300	=	4000
34	602	592	560			542		476			446	420	362			=	4000
35	602	592			556		524	476	468			420	362			=	4000
36	602		560	558		542	524		468		446				300	=	4000
37	602			558	556		524	476	468	460				356		=	4000
38	602				556			476	468	460		420	362	356	300	=	4000
39		592	560	558			524	476	468	460			362			=	4000
40		592		558	556	542	524		468	460					300	=	4000
41		592		558	556	542	524				446	420	362			=	4000
42		592		558	556	542		476	468		446		362			=	4000
43			560	558	556		524	476		460	446	420				=	4000
44			560		556		524	476			446	420	362	356	300	=	4000
45			560			542	524	476		460		420	362	356	300	=	4000
46				558	556	542				460	446	420	362	356	300	=	4000

Numbers from the Nucleon Matrix that Correlate With Matthew 5:18

Phrase: *"until heaven and earth disappear, not the smallest letter, not the least stroke of a pen"*
Gematria = 3666

Nucleon Matrix Numbers that add to 3666:

#	696	602	592	560	558	556	542	524	476	468	460	446	420	362	356	300	=
1	696	602	592		558	556								362		300	3666
2	696	602	592					524	476				420		356		3666
3	696	602		560	558					468			420	362			3666
4	696	602		560		556			476				420		356		3666
5	696	602		560				524	476			446		362			3666
6	696	602			558		542				460	446		362			3666
7	696	602			558				476	468		446	420				3666
8	696	602				556	542	524				446				300	3666
9	696	602				556	542			468		446				356	3666
10	696		592	560	558		542							362	356		3666
11	696		592	560		556	542						420			300	3666
12	696		592	560		556					460	446			356		3666
13	696		592		558		542		476			446			356		3666
14	696		592			556		524	476		460			362			3666
15	696					556	542	524		468	460		420				3666
16		602	592	560	558			524		468				362			3666
17		602	592	560		556		524	476						356		3666
18		602	592	560		556			476		460		420				3666
19		602	592		558	556	542				460				356		3666
20		602	592		558			524	476	468		446					3666
21		602	592		558				476				420	362	356	300	3666
22		602	592			556	542			468	460	446					3666
23		602	592						476	468		446	420	362		300	3666
24		602		560	558	556			476	468		446					3666
25		602		560	558		542	524			460		420				3666
26		602		560	558		542		476	468	460						3666
27		602		560	558					468	460			362	356	300	3666
28		602		560			542	524					420	362	356	300	3666
29		602		560			542		476	468				362	356	300	3666
30		602			558			524			460	446	420		356	300	3666
31		602			558				476	468	460	446			356	300	3666
32		602					542	524	476			446	420		356	300	3666
33						556	542	524	476		460	446		362		300	3666
34						556	542	524			460	446	420	362	356		3666
35						556	542			476	468	460	446		362	356	3666

Appendix 10 Continued

Phrase: "*I tell you the truth…will be any means disappear from the Law until everything is accomplished.*" Gematria = 5718

Nucleon Matrix numbers that add to 5718:

#	696	602	592	560	558	556	542	524	476	468	460	446	420	362	356	300	=
1	696	602	592	560	558			524	476	468	460		420	362			= 5718
2	696	602	592	560		556	542	524		468	460			362	356		= 5718
3	696	602	592		558	556	542	524		468	460		420			300	= 5718
4	696	602	592			556	542	524	476	468	460	446			356		= 5718
5	696				558	556	542	524	476	468	460		420	362	356	300	= 5718
6		602	592		558	556	542	524			460	446	420	362	356	300	= 5718
7		602	592		558	556	542		476	468	460	446		362	356	300	= 5718

Phrase: "*until heaven and earth disappear*" Gematria = 2310

Nucleon Matrix numbers that add to 2310:

#	696	602	592	560	558	556	542	524	476	468	460	446	420	362	356	300	=
1	696	602	592										420				= 2310
2	696								476				420	362	356		= 2310
3		602	592	560		556											= 2310
4		602	592								460				356	300	= 2310
5		602					542					446	420			300	= 2310
6			592					524	476					362	356		= 2310
7			592						476		460		420	362			= 2310
8				560		556			476					362	356		= 2310
9					558	556			476				420			300	= 2310
10					558			524		468	460					300	= 2310
11							542	524	476	468						300	= 2310
12							542	524		468			420		356		= 2310

Phrase: "*will be any means disappear from the Law*" Gematria = 2312

Nucleon Matrix numbers that add to 2312:

#	696	602	592	560	558	556	542	524	476	468	460	446	420	362	356	300	=
1	696		592			556				468							= 2312
2		602	592	560	558												= 2312
3		602						524		468				362	356		= 2312
4		602								468	460		420	362			= 2312
5			592			556						446		362	356		= 2312
6			592				542				460			362	356		= 2312
7			592					524	476				420			300	= 2312
8			592						476	468			420		356		= 2312
9				560	558				476					362	356		= 2312
10				560		556			476				420			300	= 2312
11				560				524		468	460					300	= 2312
12				560				524				446	420	362			= 2312
13				560					476	468		446		362			= 2312
14					558	556	542								356	300	= 2312
15						556	542			468		446				300	= 2312

Appendix 10 Continued

Phrase: *"I tell you the truth…until everything is accomplished"* Gematria = 3406

Nucleon Matrix numbers that add to 3406:

#	696	602	592	560	558	556	542	524	476	468	460	446	420	362	356	300	=
1	696	602		560		556		524		468							3406
2	696	602			558					468			420	362		300	3406
3	696	602				556			476				420		356	300	3406
4	696	602						524	476			446		362		300	3406
5	696	602						524		468	460				356	300	3406
6	696	602						524				446	420	362	356		3406
7	696	602							476	468		446		362	356		3406
8	696		592	560	558			524	476								3406
9	696		592	560		556	542				460						3406
10	696		592	560		556	542				460						3406
11	696		592	560					476				420	362		300	3406
12	696		592		558		542							362	356	300	3406
13	696		592			556					460	446			356	300	3406
14	696		592				542			468		446		362		300	3406
15	696			560	558				476		460				356	300	3406
16	696			560				524			460	446	420			300	3406
17	696			560					476	468	460	446				300	3406
18	696			560						468	460	446	420		356		3406
19		602	592		558			524		468				362		300	3406
20		602	592		558				476		460			362	356		3406
21		602	592			556		524	476						356	300	3406
22		602	592			556			476		460		420			300	3406
23		602	592					524			460	446	420	362			3406
24		602	592						476	468	460	446		362			3406
25		602		560	558	556				468				362		300	3406
26		602		560		556		524				446		362	356		3406
27		602		560		556					460	446	420	362			3406
28		602		560			542	524			460			362	356		3406
29		602			558	556		524				446	420			300	3406
30		602			558	556			476	468		446				300	3406
31		602			558	556				468		446	420		356		3406
32		602			558		542	524			460		420			300	3406
33		602			558		542		476	468	460					300	3406
34		602			558		542			468	460		420		356		3406
35		602					542	524	476		460	446			356		3406
36			592	560		556			476			446	420		356		3406
37			592	560			542	524		468			420			300	3406
38			592	560			542		476		460		420		356		3406
39			592	560				524		468	460	446			356		3406

APPENDIX 11

The numbers from John 3:16 that add up to 2701, Gematria of Genesis 1:1.

1. 1845 + 450 + 296 + 62 + 48 = 2701

2. 1845 + 420 + 296 + 70 + 70 = 2701

3. 1845 + 420 + 284 + 104 + 48 = 2701

4. 1845 + 296 + 284 + 215 + 61 = 2701

5. 1845 + 296 + 215 + 104 + 70 + 62 + 61 + 48 = 2701

6. 1770 + 821 + 62 + 48 = 2701

7. 1770 + 450 + 420 + 61 = 2701

8. 1770 + 420 + 296 + 215 = 2701

9. 1770 + 420 + 284 + 104 + 62 + 61 = 2701

10. 1770 + 355 + 284 + 104 + 70 + 70 + 48 = 2701

11. 1770 + 296 + 284 + 281 + 70 = 2701

12. 1770 + 296 + 281 + 104 + 70 + 70 + 62 + 48 = 2701

13. 1305 + 991 + 296 + 61 + 48 = 2701

14. 1305 + 884 + 450 + 62 = 2701

15. 1305 + 884 + 215 + 104 + 70 + 62 + 61 = 2701

16. $1305 + 865 + 296 + 104 + 70 + 61 = 2701$

17. $1305 + 865 + 281 + 70 + 70 + 62 + 48 = 2701$

18. $1305 + 623 + 420 + 104 + 70 + 70 + 61 + 48 = 2701$

19. $1305 + 623 + 296 + 284 + 70 + 62 + 61 = 2701$

20. $1305 + 530 + 500 + 296 + 70 = 2701$

21. $1305 + 530 + 450 + 355 + 61 = 2701$

22. $1305 + 530 + 450 + 284 + 70 + 62 = 2701$

23. $1305 + 530 + 450 + 215 + 70 + 70 + 61 = 2701$

24. $1305 + 530 + 420 + 281 + 104 + 61 = 2701$

25. $1305 + 530 + 355 + 296 + 215 = 2701$

26. $1305 + 530 + 355 + 284 + 104 + 62 + 61 = 2701$

27. $1305 + 530 + 284 + 215 + 104 + 70 + 70 + 62 + 61 = 2701$

28. $1305 + 500 + 450 + 281 + 104 + 61 = 2701$

29. $1305 + 500 + 420 + 296 + 70 + 62 + 48 = 2701$

30. $1305 + 500 + 296 + 281 + 215 + 104 = 2701$

31. $1305 + 450 + 420 + 355 + 62 + 61 + 48 = 2701$

32. $1305 + 450 + 420 + 215 + 70 + 70 + 62 + 61 + 48 = 2701$

33. $1305 + 450 + 284 + 281 + 215 + 104 + 62 = 2701$

34. $1305 + 420 + 420 + 355 + 70 + 70 + 61 = 2701$

35. $1305 + 420 + 420 + 281 + 104 + 62 + 61 + 48 = 2701$

36. $1305 + 420 + 355 + 296 + 215 + 62 + 48 = 2701$

37. $1305 + 355 + 296 + 284 + 281 + 70 + 62 + 48 = 2701$

38. $1305 + 355 + 296 + 281 + 215 + 70 + 70 + 61 + 48 = 2701$

39. $991 + 884 + 530 + 296 = 2701$

40. 991 + 884 + 420 + 296 + 62 + 48 = 2701

41. 991 + 884 + 296 + 281 + 70 + 70 + 61 + 48 = 2701

42. 991 + 865 + 623 + 104 + 70 + 48 = 2701

43. 991 + 865 + 500 + 284 + 61 = 2701

44. 991 + 865 + 500 + 104 + 70 + 62 + 61 + 48 = 2701

45. 991 + 865 + 450 + 215 + 70 + 62 + 48 = 2701

46. 991 + 865 + 420 + 355 + 70 = 2701

47. 991 + 865 + 355 + 215 + 104 + 62 + 61 + 48 = 2701

48. 991 + 821 + 500 + 215 + 104 + 70 = 2701

49. 991 + 821 + 420 + 281 + 70 + 70 + 48 = 2701

50. 991 + 821 + 355 + 284 + 70 + 70 + 62 + 48 = 2701

51. 991 + 821 + 284 + 281 + 215 + 61 + 48 = 2701

52. 991 + 623 + 530 + 355 + 70 + 70 + 62 = 2701

53. 991 + 623 + 530 + 281 + 215 + 61 = 2701

54. 991 + 623 + 500 + 281 + 104 + 70 + 70 + 62 = 2701

55. 991 + 623 + 450 + 284 + 104 + 70 + 70 + 61 + 48 = 2701

56. 991 + 623 + 420 + 281 + 215 + 62 + 61 + 48 = 2701

57. 991 + 623 + 355 + 296 + 284 + 104 + 48 = 2701

58. 991 + 623 + 355 + 281 + 215 + 104 + 70 + 62 = 2701

59. 991 + 623 + 296 + 284 + 215 + 104 + 70 + 70 + 48 = 2701

60. 991 + 530 + 500 + 355 + 215 + 62 + 48 = 2701

61. 991 + 530 + 450 + 284 + 281 + 104 + 61 = 2701

62. 991 + 530 + 420 + 355 + 296 + 61 + 48 = 2701

63. 991 + 530 + 420 + 296 + 284 + 70 + 62 + 48 = 2701

64. $991 + 530 + 420 + 296 + 215 + 70 + 70 + 61 + 48 = 2701$

65. $991 + 530 + 296 + 284 + 281 + 215 + 104 = 2701$

66. $991 + 500 + 450 + 355 + 296 + 61 + 48 = 2701$

67. $991 + 500 + 450 + 296 + 284 + 70 + 62 + 48 = 2701$

68. $991 + 500 + 450 + 296 + 215 + 70 + 70 + 61 + 48 = 2701$

69. $991 + 500 + 420 + 296 + 281 + 104 + 61 + 48 = 2701$

70. $991 + 500 + 355 + 296 + 284 + 104 + 62 + 61 + 48 = 2701$

71. $991 + 500 + 296 + 284 + 215 + 104 + 70 + 70 + 62 + 61 + 48 = 2701$

72. $991 + 450 + 420 + 420 + 420 = 2701$

73. $991 + 450 + 420 + 355 + 284 + 70 + 70 + 61 = 2701$

74. $991 + 450 + 420 + 296 + 281 + 215 + 48 = 2701$

75. $991 + 450 + 420 + 296 + 281 + 70 + 70 + 62 + 61 = 2701$

76. $991 + 450 + 420 + 284 + 281 + 104 + 62 + 61 + 48 = 2701$

77. $991 + 450 + 355 + 296 + 284 + 215 + 62 + 48 = 2701$

78. $991 + 420 + 420 + 420 + 284 + 104 + 62 = 2701$

79. $991 + 420 + 420 + 420 + 215 + 104 + 70 + 61 = 2701$

80. $991 + 420 + 420 + 284 + 281 + 104 + 70 + 70 + 61 = 2701$

81. $991 + 420 + 355 + 296 + 284 + 215 + 70 + 70 = 2701$

82. $991 + 420 + 296 + 284 + 281 + 215 + 104 + 62 + 48 = 2701$

83. $884 + 865 + 821 + 70 + 61 = 2701$

84. $884 + 865 + 623 + 281 + 48 = 2701$

85. $884 + 865 + 500 + 281 + 62 + 61 + 48 = 2701$

86. $884 + 865 + 420 + 296 + 104 + 70 + 62 = 2701$

87. $884 + 821 + 500 + 281 + 215 = 2701$

88. 884 + 821 + 450 + 296 + 70 + 70 + 62 + 48 = 2701

89. 884 + 821 + 420 + 284 + 104 + 70 + 70 + 48 = 2701

90. 884 + 821 + 355 + 296 + 284 + 61 = 2701

91. 884 + 821 + 355 + 296 + 104 + 70 + 62 + 61 + 48 = 2701

92. 884 + 821 + 296 + 284 + 215 + 70 + 70 + 61 = 2701

93. 884 + 623 + 530 + 450 + 104 + 62 + 48 = 2701

94. 884 + 623 + 530 + 420 + 104 + 70 + 70 = 2701

95. 884 + 623 + 530 + 284 + 215 + 104 + 61 = 2701

96. 884 + 623 + 500 + 450 + 104 + 70 + 70 = 2701

97. 884 + 623 + 450 + 420 + 215 + 61 + 48 = 2701

98. 884 + 623 + 450 + 355 + 215 + 104 + 70 = 2701

99. 884 + 623 + 450 + 284 + 281 + 70 + 61 + 48 = 2701

100. 884 + 623 + 420 + 420 + 284 + 70 = 2701

101. 884 + 623 + 420 + 420 + 104 + 70 + 70 + 62 + 48 = 2701

102. 884 + 623 + 420 + 355 + 296 + 62 + 61 = 2701

103. 884 + 623 + 420 + 296 + 215 + 70 + 70 + 62 + 61 = 2701

104. 884 + 623 + 420 + 284 + 215 + 104 + 62 + 61 + 48 = 2701

105. 884 + 623 + 296 + 284 + 281 + 215 + 70 + 48 = 2701

106. 884 + 530 + 500 + 420 + 215 + 104 + 48 = 2701

107. 884 + 530 + 500 + 420 + 104 + 70 + 70 + 62 + 61 = 2701

108. 884 + 530 + 500 + 284 + 281 + 104 + 70 + 48 = 2701

109. 884 + 530 + 450 + 420 + 355 + 62 = 2701

110. 884 + 530 + 450 + 420 + 215 + 70 + 70 + 62 = 2701

111. 884 + 530 + 450 + 355 + 281 + 70 + 70 + 61 = 2701

112. $884 + 530 + 420 + 420 + 281 + 104 + 62 = 2701$

113. $884 + 530 + 420 + 355 + 215 + 104 + 70 + 62 + 61 = 2701$

114. $884 + 530 + 355 + 296 + 281 + 215 + 70 + 70 = 2701$

115. $884 + 530 + 355 + 284 + 281 + 215 + 104 + 48 = 2701$

116. $884 + 530 + 355 + 284 + 281 + 104 + 70 + 70 + 62 + 61 = 2701$

117. $884 + 500 + 450 + 420 + 281 + 104 + 62 = 2701$

118. $884 + 500 + 450 + 355 + 215 + 104 + 70 + 62 + 61 = 2701$

119. $884 + 500 + 420 + 420 + 284 + 70 + 62 + 61 = 2701$

120. $884 + 500 + 296 + 284 + 281 + 215 + 70 + 62 + 61 + 48 = 2701$

121. $884 + 450 + 420 + 355 + 281 + 70 + 70 + 62 + 61 + 48 = 2701$

122. $884 + 450 + 420 + 296 + 284 + 215 + 104 + 48 = 2701$

123. $884 + 450 + 420 + 296 + 284 + 104 + 70 + 70 + 62 + 61 = 2701$

124. $884 + 420 + 420 + 420 + 355 + 70 + 70 + 62 = 2701$

125. $884 + 420 + 420 + 420 + 281 + 215 + 61 = 2701$

126. $884 + 420 + 420 + 355 + 284 + 215 + 62 + 61 = 2701$

127. $884 + 420 + 355 + 296 + 281 + 215 + 70 + 70 + 62 + 48 = 2701$

128. $865 + 821 + 530 + 284 + 70 + 70 + 61 = 2701$

129. $865 + 821 + 450 + 284 + 281 = 2701$

130. $865 + 821 + 450 + 281 + 104 + 70 + 62 + 48 = 2701$

131. $865 + 821 + 420 + 284 + 70 + 70 + 62 + 61 + 48 = 2701$

132. $865 + 821 + 284 + 281 + 215 + 104 + 70 + 61 = 2701$

133. $865 + 623 + 530 + 420 + 215 + 48 = 2701$

134. $865 + 623 + 530 + 420 + 70 + 70 + 62 + 61 = 2701$

135. $865 + 623 + 530 + 284 + 281 + 70 + 48 = 2701$

136. $865 + 623 + 500 + 450 + 215 + 48 = 2701$

137. $865 + 623 + 500 + 450 + 70 + 70 + 62 + 61 = 2701$

138. $865 + 623 + 500 + 355 + 296 + 62 = 2701$

139. $865 + 623 + 500 + 296 + 215 + 70 + 70 + 62 = 2701$

140. $865 + 623 + 500 + 284 + 215 + 104 + 62 + 48 = 2701$

141. $865 + 623 + 450 + 420 + 281 + 62 = 2701$

142. $865 + 623 + 450 + 355 + 215 + 70 + 62 + 61 = 2701$

143. $865 + 623 + 420 + 296 + 284 + 104 + 61 + 48 = 2701$

144. $865 + 623 + 420 + 281 + 215 + 104 + 70 + 62 + 61 = 2701$

145. $865 + 530 + 500 + 420 + 215 + 62 + 61 + 48 = 2701$

146. $865 + 530 + 500 + 355 + 215 + 104 + 70 + 62 = 2701$

147. $865 + 530 + 500 + 284 + 281 + 70 + 62 + 61 + 48 = 2701$

148. $865 + 530 + 450 + 420 + 296 + 70 + 70 = 2701$

149. $865 + 530 + 450 + 420 + 284 + 104 + 48 = 2701$

150. $865 + 530 + 450 + 296 + 284 + 215 + 61 = 2701$

151. $865 + 530 + 450 + 296 + 215 + 104 + 70 + 62 + 61 + 48 = 2701$

152. $865 + 530 + 420 + 355 + 296 + 104 + 70 + 61 = 2701$

153. $865 + 530 + 420 + 355 + 281 + 70 + 70 + 62 + 48 = 2701$

154. $865 + 530 + 420 + 296 + 284 + 104 + 70 + 70 + 62 = 2701$

155. $865 + 530 + 355 + 284 + 281 + 215 + 62 + 61 + 48 = 2701$

156. $865 + 500 + 450 + 355 + 296 + 104 + 70 + 61 = 2701$

157. $865 + 500 + 450 + 355 + 281 + 70 + 70 + 62 + 48 = 2701$

158. $865 + 500 + 450 + 296 + 284 + 104 + 70 + 70 + 62 = 2701$

159. $865 + 500 + 420 + 420 + 281 + 215 = 2701$

160. $865 + 500 + 420 + 355 + 284 + 215 + 62 = 2701$

161. $865 + 500 + 355 + 284 + 281 + 215 + 70 + 70 + 61 = 2701$

162. $865 + 450 + 420 + 420 + 296 + 70 + 70 + 62 + 48 = 2701$

163. $865 + 450 + 420 + 296 + 284 + 215 + 62 + 61 + 48 = 2701$

164. $865 + 450 + 420 + 296 + 281 + 215 + 104 + 70 = 2701$

165. $865 + 450 + 355 + 296 + 284 + 215 + 104 + 70 + 62 = 2701$

166. $865 + 420 + 420 + 420 + 284 + 104 + 70 + 70 + 48 = 2701$

167. $865 + 420 + 420 + 355 + 296 + 284 + 61 = 2701$

168. $865 + 420 + 420 + 355 + 296 + 104 + 70 + 62 + 61 + 48 = 2701$

169. $865 + 420 + 420 + 296 + 284 + 215 + 70 + 70 + 61 = 2701$

170. $821 + 623 + 530 + 500 + 104 + 62 + 61 = 2701$

171. $821 + 623 + 530 + 450 + 215 + 62 = 2701$

172. $821 + 623 + 500 + 355 + 284 + 70 + 48 = 2701$

173. $821 + 623 + 500 + 296 + 281 + 70 + 62 + 48 = 2701$

174. $821 + 623 + 450 + 355 + 281 + 62 + 61 + 48 = 2701$

175. $821 + 623 + 450 + 296 + 284 + 104 + 62 + 61 = 2701$

176. $821 + 623 + 450 + 281 + 215 + 70 + 70 + 62 + 61 + 48 = 2701$

177. $821 + 623 + 420 + 420 + 355 + 62 = 2701$

178. $821 + 623 + 420 + 420 + 215 + 70 + 70 + 62 = 2701$

179. $821 + 623 + 420 + 355 + 281 + 70 + 70 + 61 = 2701$

180. $821 + 623 + 355 + 296 + 281 + 215 + 62 + 48 = 2701$

181. $821 + 530 + 500 + 450 + 296 + 104 = 2701$

182. $821 + 530 + 500 + 355 + 281 + 104 + 62 + 48 = 2701$

183. $821 + 530 + 500 + 284 + 281 + 215 + 70 = 2701$

184. $821 + 530 + 500 + 281 + 215 + 104 + 70 + 70 + 62 + 48 = 2701$

185. $821 + 530 + 450 + 355 + 296 + 70 + 70 + 61 + 48 = 2701$

186. $821 + 530 + 420 + 420 + 296 + 104 + 62 + 48 = 2701$

187. $821 + 530 + 420 + 296 + 281 + 104 + 70 + 70 + 61 + 48 = 2701$

188. $821 + 530 + 355 + 296 + 284 + 104 + 70 + 70 + 62 + 61 + 48 = 2701$

189. $821 + 500 + 450 + 420 + 296 + 104 + 62 + 48 = 2701$

190. $821 + 500 + 450 + 296 + 281 + 104 + 70 + 70 + 61 + 48 = 2701$

191. $821 + 500 + 420 + 420 + 296 + 104 + 70 + 70 = 2701$

192. $821 + 500 + 420 + 355 + 281 + 215 + 61 + 48 = 2701$

193. $821 + 500 + 420 + 296 + 284 + 215 + 104 + 61 = 2701$

194. $821 + 500 + 420 + 284 + 281 + 215 + 70 + 62 + 48 = 2701$

195. $821 + 450 + 420 + 420 + 355 + 104 + 70 + 61 = 2701$

196. $821 + 450 + 420 + 420 + 284 + 104 + 70 + 70 + 62 = 2701$

197. $821 + 450 + 355 + 296 + 284 + 281 + 104 + 62 + 48 = 2701$

198. $821 + 450 + 355 + 296 + 281 + 215 + 104 + 70 + 61 + 48 = 2701$

199. $821 + 450 + 296 + 284 + 281 + 215 + 104 + 70 + 70 + 62 + 48 = 2701$

200. $821 + 420 + 420 + 420 + 296 + 215 + 61 + 48 = 2701$

201. $821 + 420 + 420 + 355 + 296 + 215 + 104 + 70 = 2701$

202. $821 + 420 + 420 + 296 + 284 + 281 + 70 + 61 + 48 = 2701$

203. $821 + 420 + 355 + 296 + 284 + 281 + 104 + 70 + 70 = 2701$

204. $623 + 530 + 500 + 420 + 296 + 284 + 48 = 2701$

205. $623 + 530 + 500 + 420 + 281 + 215 + 70 + 62 = 2701$

206. $623 + 530 + 450 + 420 + 284 + 215 + 70 + 61 + 48 = 2701$

207. $623 + 530 + 450 + 355 + 296 + 281 + 104 + 62 = 2701$

208. $623 + 530 + 450 + 355 + 284 + 215 + 104 + 70 + 70 = 2701$

209. $623 + 530 + 450 + 296 + 281 + 215 + 104 + 70 + 70 + 62 = 2701$

210. $623 + 530 + 420 + 420 + 355 + 104 + 70 + 70 + 61 + 48 = 2701$

211. $623 + 530 + 420 + 420 + 296 + 281 + 70 + 61 = 2701$

212. $623 + 530 + 420 + 355 + 296 + 284 + 70 + 62 + 61 = 2701$

213. $623 + 500 + 450 + 420 + 355 + 104 + 70 + 70 + 61 + 48 = 2701$

214. $623 + 500 + 450 + 420 + 296 + 281 + 70 + 61 = 2701$

215. $623 + 500 + 450 + 355 + 296 + 284 + 70 + 62 + 61 = 2701$

216. $623 + 500 + 420 + 420 + 296 + 215 + 104 + 62 + 61 = 2701$

217. $623 + 500 + 420 + 355 + 296 + 215 + 104 + 70 + 70 + 48 = 2701$

218. $623 + 500 + 420 + 296 + 284 + 281 + 104 + 70 + 62 + 61 = 2701$

219. $623 + 450 + 420 + 420 + 355 + 281 + 104 + 48 = 2701$

220. $623 + 450 + 420 + 420 + 281 + 215 + 104 + 70 + 70 + 48 = 2701$

221. $623 + 450 + 420 + 355 + 296 + 281 + 215 + 61 = 2701$

222. $623 + 450 + 420 + 355 + 284 + 215 + 104 + 70 + 70 + 62 + 48 = 2701$

223. 623 + 450 + 420 + 296 + 284 + 281 + 215 + 70 + 62 = 2701

224. 623 + 420 + 420 + 420 + 355 + 284 + 70 + 61 + 48 = 2701

225. 623 + 420 + 420 + 420 + 296 + 281 + 70 + 62 + 61 + 48 = 2701

226. 623 + 420 + 420 + 355 + 296 + 281 + 104 + 70 + 70 + 62 = 2701

227. 623 + 420 + 355 + 296 + 284 + 281 + 215 + 104 + 62 + 61 = 2701

228. 530 + 500 + 450 + 420 + 420 + 215 + 104 + 62 = 2701

229. 530 + 500 + 450 + 420 + 355 + 281 + 104 + 61 = 2701

230. 530 + 500 + 450 + 420 + 284 + 281 + 104 + 70 + 62 = 2701

231. 530 + 500 + 450 + 420 + 281 + 215 + 104 + 70 + 70 + 61 = 2701

232. 530 + 500 + 450 + 355 + 284 + 215 + 104 + 70 + 70 + 62 + 61 = 2701

233. 530 + 500 + 420 + 420 + 355 + 296 + 70 + 62 + 48 = 2701

234. 530 + 500 + 420 + 355 + 296 + 281 + 215 + 104 = 2701

235. 530 + 450 + 420 + 420 + 420 + 296 + 104 + 61 = 2701

236. 530 + 450 + 420 + 420 + 420 + 281 + 70 + 62 + 48 = 2701

237. 530 + 450 + 420 + 420 + 355 + 215 + 70 + 70 + 62 + 61 + 48 = 2701

238. 530 + 450 + 420 + 355 + 284 + 281 + 215 + 104 + 62 = 2701

239. 530 + 420 + 420 + 420 + 355 + 281 + 104 + 62 + 61 + 48 = 2701

240. 530 + 420 + 420 + 420 + 284 + 281 + 215 + 70 + 61 = 2701

241. 530 + 420 + 420 + 420 + 281 + 215 + 104 + 70 + 70 + 62 + 61 +48 = 2701

242. 500 + 450 + 420 + 420 + 355 + 281 + 104 + 62 + 61 + 48 = 2701

243. 243. $500 + 450 + 420 + 420 + 284 + 281 + 215 + 70 + 61 = 2701$

244. $500 + 450 + 420 + 420 + 281 + 215 + 104 + 70 + 70 + 62 + 61 + 48 = 2701$

245. $500 + 420 + 420 + 420 + 355 + 281 + 104 + 70 + 70 + 61 = 2701$

246. $500 + 420 + 420 + 355 + 296 + 281 + 215 + 104 + 62 + 48 = 2701$

247. $450 + 420 + 420 + 420 + 355 + 281 + 215 + 70 + 70 = 2701$

248. $420 + 420 + 420 + 355 + 284 + 281 + 215 + 104 + 70 + 70 + 62 = 2701$

APPENDIX 12

Prophecies Concerning History from Babylonian Empire to Nearly Time of Christ From Daniel 11

Number	Scripture	Prophecy	Fulfillment
1	Daniel 11:2	Three more kings will appear in Persia	Cambyses II (530-522 BC), Pseudo-Smerdis or Gaumata (522), Darius I (522-486)
2	Daniel 11:2	Fourth king richer than the others will stir up everyone against kingdom of Greece	Xerxes I (486-465) attempted to conquer Greece in 480 BC
3	Daniel 11:3	Then a mighty king will appear, who will rule with great power and do as he pleases.	Alexander the Great (336-323 BC)
4	Daniel 11:4	His empire will be broken up and parceled out toward the four winds of heaven. It will not go to his descendants...	Empire divided among Alexander's four generals: Lysimachus, Cassander, Ptolemy I, Seleucos I
5	Daniel 11:5	King of South will become strong	Ptolemy I Soter (323-285 BC) founded the Ptolemaic Dynasty
6	Daniel 11:5	One of his own commanders will become stronger and rule his own kingdom.	Seleucus I Nacator (311-280 BC) founded the Seleucid Dynasty (the north)
7	Daniel 11:6	The daughter of the king of South will go to the king of the North to make an alliance	Bereneice, daughter of Ptolemy II Philadelphus (285-246 BC) married Antiochus II Theos (261-246 BC)
8	Daniel 11:6	She will not retain her power, and he and his power will not last.	Antiochus's former wife, Laodice, conspired to have Berenice and Antiochus put to death.
9	Daniel 11:6	She will be handed over, together with her royal escort and her father	Berenice's father Ptolemy died 246 BC.
10	Daniel 11:7	One from her family line will arise to take her place.	Berenice's brother, Ptolemy III Euergetes (246-222 BC) killed Laodice.
11	Daniel 11:7	He will attack King of the North and be victorious.	Ptolemy III attacked king of the north, Seleucus II Callinicus (246-226BC) and took over fortress in Antioch.
12	Daniel 11:8	He will seize their gods ... and their valuable articles of silver and gold and take them to Egypt. For some years he will leave the king of the North alone.	Ptolemy III returned to Egypt in 245 BC taking with him 40,000 talents of gold and the statues of Egyptian gods. In 241 BC Ptolemy made peace with the Seleucids
13	Daniel 11:9	Then the king of the North will invade the realm of the king of the South but will retreat to his own country.	Seleucus II still king of the North at this time.

Appendix 12 Continued

14	Daniel 11:10	His sons will prepare for war... which will sweep on like an irresistible flood and carry the battle as far as his fortress.	Two sons were Seleucus II Ceraunus (226-223 BC) and Antiochus III (the Great) (223-187 BC). The fortress was Ptolemy's fortress at Raphia in southern Palestine.
15	Daniel 11:11	Then the king of the South will march out in a rage and fight against the king of the North, who ... will be defeated	King of the South Ptolemy IV Philopator (221-203 BC) of Egypt defeated king of the North, Antiochus III at Raphia in 217 BC.
16	Daniel 11:12	When the army is carried off, the king of the South will ... slaughter many thousands.	The historian Polybius records that Antiochus lost nearly 10,000 infantrymen at Raphia.
17	Daniel 11:13	King of the North will muster another army, larger than the first... after several years he will advance with a huge army fully equipped.	During the Fifth Syrian War (202-195 BC) Antiochus III conquered the Ptolemies' territories in Asia Minor and invaded Palestine in 201 BC.
18	Daniel 11:14	Many will rise against the king of the South. The violent men among your own people will rebel... but without success.	Jews joined forces with Antiochus, but the Ptolemaic general Scopas crushed the rebellion in 200 BC.
19	Daniel 11:15	Then the king of the North will come and build up siege ramps and will capture a fortified city. The forces of the South will be powerless to resist.	Antiochus III defeated the Ptolemies at the Battle of Panium (200 BC) near the head of the River Jordan. He also captured the Mediterranean port of Sidon.
20	Daniel 11:16	The invader... will establish himself in the Beautiful Land and will have the power to destroy it.	Antiochus was in control of Palestine (formerly Israel) by 197 BC.
21	Daniel 11:17	He will make an alliance with the king of the South. And he will give him a daughter in marriage in order to overthrow the kingdom, but his plans will not succeed.	Antiochus gave his daughter Cleopatra I in marriage to Ptolemy V in 193 BC.
22	Daniel 11:18	Then he will turn his attention to the coastlands and will take many of them.	Antiochus III attacked secured coast towns and independent Greek cities. He invaded mainland Greece in 192 BC.
23	Daniel 11:18	but a commander will put an end to his insolence and will turn his insolence back upon him.	The Roman consul Lucius Cornelius Scipio Asiaticus, defeated Antiochus III at Magnesia in Asia Minor in 190 B.C.

Appendix 12 Continued

24	Daniel 11:19	After this, he will turn back toward the fortresses of his own country but will stumble and fall to be seen no more.	Antiochus died in 187 B.C. while attempting to plunder a temple in the province of Elymais.
25	Daniel 11:20	His successor will send out a tax collector to maintain the royal splendor.	Antiochus's son was Seleucus IV Philopator (187-175 B.C.) Seleucus's finance minister was Heliodorus.
26	Daniel 11:20	In a few years...he will be destroyed, yet not in anger or in battle.	Heliodorus conspired against Seleucus and had him killed.
27	Daniel 11:21	He will be succeeded by a contemptible person who has not been given honor of royalty...He will seize it through intrigue.	Seleucus's younger brother Antiochus IV Epiphanes (175-164 B.C.) seized power although the rightful heir to the throne was Seleucus's young son (later to become Demetrius I).
28	Daniel 11:22	Then an overwhelming army will be swept away before him; both it and a prince of the covenant will be destroyed.	The "prince of the covenant" is the high priest Onias III who was murdered in 170 B.C.
29	Daniel 11:23	After coming to an agreement with him, he will act deceitfully, and with only a few people he will rise to power.	The legitimate heir, Demetrius I Soter, replaced Antiochus as a hostage in Rome and with the help of King Eumenes II of Pergamum, Antiochus IV traveled to Syria and seized the throne in November 175 BC.
30	Daniel 11:24	When the richest provinces feel secure, he will invade them and will achieve what neither his fathers nor his forefathers did.	In the Sixth Syrian War, Antiochus IV conquered Cyprus and large parts of Egypt, something the Seleucids had not previously accomplished.
31	Daniel 11:25	With a large army he will invade king of the South...who will not be able to stand because of the plots devised against him.	Antiochus IV invaded Egypt in 170 BC, conquering all but Alexandria and capturing King Ptolemy (king of the South).
32	Daniel 11:27	The two kings...will sit at the same table and lie to each other.	Perhaps Antiochus IV and Ptolemy VI after Antiochus captured him or Ptolemy VI and Ptolemy VIII who were brothers and in conflict with each other over the throne.

Appendix 12 Continued

33	Daniel 11:28	The king of the North will return to his own country with great wealth, but his heart will be set against the holy covenant. He will take action against it and then return to his own country.	After Antiochus IV victory in Egypt, he returned to Syria. Enroute, he plundered the temple in Jerusalem in 169 B.C., set up a garrison there and massacred many Jews in the city.
34	Daniel 11:29 - 11:30	He will invade the South again, but ...ships of the western coastlands will oppose him and he will lose heart	In 168 BC Antiochus IV led a second attack on Egypt, but Romans sailed to Alexandria before he arrived and Roman Ambassador Gaius Popillius Laenas gave message that Rome would attack Antiochus if he didn't leave Egypt. Antiochus decided to return to Syria, fearing the Romans.
35	Daniel 11:30 - 11:31	Then he will turn back and vent his fury against the holy covenant. His armed forces will rise up to desecrate the temple...they will set up the abomination that causes desolation.	Antiochus Epiphanes slaughtered thousands of Jews in Jerusalem and set up an altar to the pagan god Zeus Olympius in the temple in Jerusalem in 168 BC.
36	Daniel 11:33	Those who are wise will instruct many, though for a time they will fall by the sword or be burned or captured or plundered.	The godly leaders of the Jewish resistance movement were called the Hasidim. Their persecution of the Jews at that time was severe.
37	Daniel 11:34	When they fall, they will receive a little help.	Mattathias, a Jewish priest, and his son Judas Maccabeus (Judah Maccabee) led the Maccabean Revolt against the Seleucid Empire. The Jewish holiday of Hanukkah commemorates the restoration of Jewish worship at the temple in Jerusalem in 164 BC, after Judah removed all of the statues depicting Greek gods and goddesses and purified it.

CHAPTER NOTES

Introduction

1. "The Astonishing Pattern of SEVENS in Genesis 1:1", https:// www. biblebelievers.org.au/panin3.htm
2. "Ivan Panin", https://en.wikipedia.org/wiki/Ivan Panin#Biography
3. "The Historical Reliability of the New Testament Text", https:// www. growthtrac.com
4. "Scripture Access Statistics", https://www.wycliffe.net/resources/ statistics/

Section 1, Chapter 1

1. "Hindu-Arabic numerals | History & Facts | Britannica.com", https:// www.britannica.com/topic/Hindu-Arabic-numerals
2. From answers.yahoo.com, "What Greek letter corresponds to the number six?" https://answers.yahoo.com/question/index?qid= 20140605175558AAGHFgs
3. Letter Number Equivalent in Languages in the Bible, https://www. agapebiblestudy.com

Section 1, Chapter 2

1. All quoted English scripture in the text of this book is from *The NIV StudyBible New International Version*, Zondervan Bible Publishers, 1985, unless otherwise noted.
2. Hebrew text here and throughout book is copied from Unicode XML Leningrad Codex (UXLC 1.0) at www.tanach.us/

3. Nuyten, John, "Hidden Code in Genesis 1:1", https://www. thelivingword.org.au/grand-design/session10.php

4. Tavares, Leo, "Ordinal Genesis 1:1/John 1:1 Triangle", https://site/ mathematicalmonotheism/ordinal-genesis-1-1-john-1-1-triangle

5. Historical Archive of the Bible Wheel Site, Full Text Hebrew/ Greek Bible Gematria Database, https://www.biblewheel.com/GR/ GR Database.php?Gem Number=37&SearchByNum=Go

6. Nuyten, John, "37 and 73", https://www.thelivingword.org.au/ granddesign/session14.php

7. Bluer, Peter, "Bible Numerics Part 3, YouTube June 5, 2010

8. "A Brief History of Pi", https://www.exploratorium.edu/pi/ history-of-pi

Section 1, Chapter 3

1. Nuyten, John: LivingGreekNT.org

2. Bluer Peter, "Bible Numerics Part 3", YouTube June 5, 2010

3. "e (mathematical constant), https://en.wikipedia.org/wiki/E (mathematical constant)

Section 1, Chapter 4

1. Bluer Peter, "Bible Numerics Part 4", YouTube April 13, 2009

Section 1, Chapter 7

1. Colossians 1:17 Greek words and numerical equivalent come from Nuyten, John: LivingGreekNT.org. Similarly, all New Testament verses later in the book with listed Greek words and numerical equivalents are pulled from LivingGreekNT.org.

Section 1, Chapter 9

1. I counted the number of words using the Unicode/XML Leningrad Codex. Some words in Hebrew are joined by a hyphen. The first occurrence of this joining of words is in Genesis 1:2 with the two Hebrew words: עַל־פְּנֵי If two Hebrew words were joined by a hyphen, then I counted it as two words, not one word. In Genesis 1 there are also a few combinations of three words connected by a hyphen. The first occurrence of this three-word connection is in Genesis 1:29 אֶת־כָּל־עֵשֶׂב This grouping is counted as three words.
2. Nuyten, John, https://www.livinggreeknt.org/NTbooks/revelation/revelation22.php. Also on the Home Page bottom right column of https://www.livinggreeknt.org.

Section 2, Chapter 10

1. Modified from *The NIV Study Bible New International Version,* Zondervan Bible Publishers, 1985, Identification of the Four Kingdoms diagram, pg 1311.
2. Cyrus the Great – Wikipedia, https://en.wikipedia.org/wiki/ Cyrus the Great
3. Cambyses II – Wikipedia, https://en.wikipedia.org/wiki/Cambyses_II
4. Darius the Great – Wikipedia, https://en.wikipedia.org/wiki/ Darius I
5. Gaumata / Smerdis, Livius.org, https://www.livius.org/articles/ person/gaumata-smerdis/
6. Xerxes I Biography, Accomplishments, & Facts, Britannica, https://www. britannica.com/biography/Xerxes-I
7. Artaxerxes – Ancient History Encyclopedia, https://www.ancient. eu/ Artaxerxes I
8. Xerxes II, Encyclopedia.com, https://www.encyclopedia.com/ reference/ encyclopedias-almanacs-transcripts-and-maps/xerxes-ii
9. Darius II – Wikipedia, https://en.wikipedia.org/wiki/Darius II
10. Artaxerxes II of Persia – Wikipedia, https://en.wikipedia.org/wiki/ Artaxerxes II
11. Artaxerxes III –Wikipedia, https://en.wikipedia.org/wiki/ Artaxerxes III

12. Arses (November 338-June 336 BC), www.historyofwar.org/arti- cles/people arses.html

13. Darius III – Wikipedia, https://en.wikipedia.org/wiki/Darius III

14. Alexander the Great –Wikipedia, https://en.wikipedia.org/wiki/Alexander the Great

15. Ptolemy I Soter, Macedonian King of Egypt, Britannica, https:// www.britannica.com/biography/Ptolemy-I-Soter

16. The Seleucid Empire after Alexander the Great: Anatolia and Beyond, Brewminate, https://brewminate.com/the-seleucid-empir e-after-alexander-the-great-anatolia-and-beyond/

17. Berenice Daughter of Ptolemy II, Encyclopaedia Britannica, https:// www.britannica.com/biography/Berenice-daughter-of-Ptolemy-II

18. Laodice I, Wikipedia, https://en.wikipedia.org/wiki/Laodice I

19. Ptolemy II Philadelphus, Britannica, https://www.britannica.com/biography/Ptolemy-II-Philadelphus

20. Seleucus II Callinicus, Wikipedia, https://en.wikipedia.org/wiki/Seleucus II Callinicus

21. Laodice I, Wikipedia, https://en.wikipedia.org/wiki/Laodice I

22. Ptolemy III Euergetes, Wikipedia, https://en.wikipedia.org/wiki/Ptolemy III Euergetes

23. Seluecus III Ceraunus, Wikipedia, https://en.wikipedia.org/wiki/Seleucus III Ceraunus

24. Antiochus III the Great, Wikipedia, https://en.wikipedia.org/wiki/Antiochus III the Great

25. Battle of Raphia, Wikipedia, https://en.wikipedia.org/wiki/Battle of Raphia

26. Ptolemy V Epiphanes, FifthSyriaWar, Wikipedia, https://en.wikipedia.org/wiki/PtolemyV Epiphanes#Fifth Syrian War (202-196 BC

27. Syrian Wars, Fifth Syrian War, Wikipedia, https://en.wikipedia.org/wiki/Syrian Wars#Fifth Syrian War .28202-195 BC.29

28. NIV Study Bible, Zondervan Bible Publishers, 1985, Study note for Daniel 11:16.

29. Cleopatra I Syra, Wikipedia, https://en.wikipedia.org/wiki/Cleopatra I Syra

30. Antiochus III the Great, Wikipedia, War against Rome, https://en.wikipedia.org/wiki/Antiochus III the Great

31. Treaty of Apamea, Wikipedia, https://en.wikipedia.org/wiki/Treaty of Apamea

32. Seleucus IV Philopator, Wikipedia, Taxes and assassination, https://en.wikipedia.org/wiki/Seleucus IV Philopator

33. Antiochus IV Epiphanes, Wikipedia, Wars Against Egypt and Relations with Rome, https://en.wikipedia.org/wiki/ Antiochus IV Epiphanes

34. Onias III, Wikipedia, https://en.wikipedia.org/wiki/Onias III

35. Antiochus IV Epiphanes, Wikipedia, Rise to Power, https://en.wikipedia.org/wiki/Antiochus IV Epiphanes

36. Antiochus IV Epiphanes, Main Deeds, Livius.org, https://www. livius.org/articles/person/antiochus-iv-epiphanes/

37. Ptolemy VI Philometor, Wikipedia, https://en.wikipedia.org/wiki/ Ptolemy VI Philometor

38. NIV Study Bible, Zondervan Bible Publishers, 1985, Study note for Daniel 11:28.

39. 1 Maccabees 1:54, 59; 2 Maccabees 6:2

40. Maccabean Revolt, Wikipedia, https://wikipedia.org/wiki/Maccabean Revolt

41. NIV Study Bible, Zondervan Bible Publishers, 1985, Study note for Daniel 11:36

Section 3, Chapter 13

1. "Blast from the past: Dead woman raised back to life by Elijah Challenge-trained disciples before astonished Muslims", Oct 13, 2019, "https://theelijahchallenge.org/dead-woman-raised-back-life-lords-disciples-issue-command-jesus-name/"

Appendix 1

1. "Aramaic: The Bible's third language", https://truthonlybible.com/2015/11/23/aramaic-the-bibles-third-language/

2. Parsons, John J., <u>A Year Through the Torah—A Week-By-Week Journey for Christians</u>, Hebrew Heart Publications, Scottsdale, Arizona, pg. 1

3. "Jewish Languages: From Aramaic to Yiddish", https://www.myjewishlearning.com/article/jewish-languages-from-aramaic-to-yiddish

4. McCall, Thomas S., "The Language of the Gospel", Zola Levitt Ministries, https://www.levitt.com/essays/language

CPSIA information can be obtained
at www.ICGtesting.com
Printed in the USA
LVHW010106100721
692231LV00001B/1

9 781648 303661